Library of
Davidson College

# What Does Revelation Mean for the Modern Jew?

## Rosenzweig, Buber, Fackenheim

by
**MICHAEL OPPENHEIM**

Symposium Series
Volume 17

The Edwin Mellen Press
Lewiston/Queenston

**Library of Congress Cataloging-in-Publication Data**

Oppenheim, Michael D., 1946-
   What does Revelation mean for the modern Jew?

   (Symposium series ; v. 17)
   Bibliography: p.
   **Includes index.**
   1. Revelation (Jewish theology)--History of doctrines.
2. Rosenzweig, Franz, 1886-1929. 3. Buber, Martin,
1878-1965. 4. Fackenheim, Emil L. I. Title.
II. Series: Symposium series (Edwin Mellen Press)
BM645.R5066  1985       296.3'11        85-18929
ISBN 0-88946-708-0 (alk. paper)

> This is volume 17 in the continuing series
> Symposium Series
> Volume 17 ISBN 0-88946-708-0
> SS Series ISBN 0-88946-989-X

Copyright © 1985, The Edwin Mellen Press

All rights reserved. For more information contact

The Edwin Mellen Press           The Edwin Mellen Press
Box 450                                            Box 67
Lewiston, New York               Queenston, Ontario
USA  14092                              L0S 1L0  CANADA

Printed in the United States of America

*For Martha, David, and Aaron*

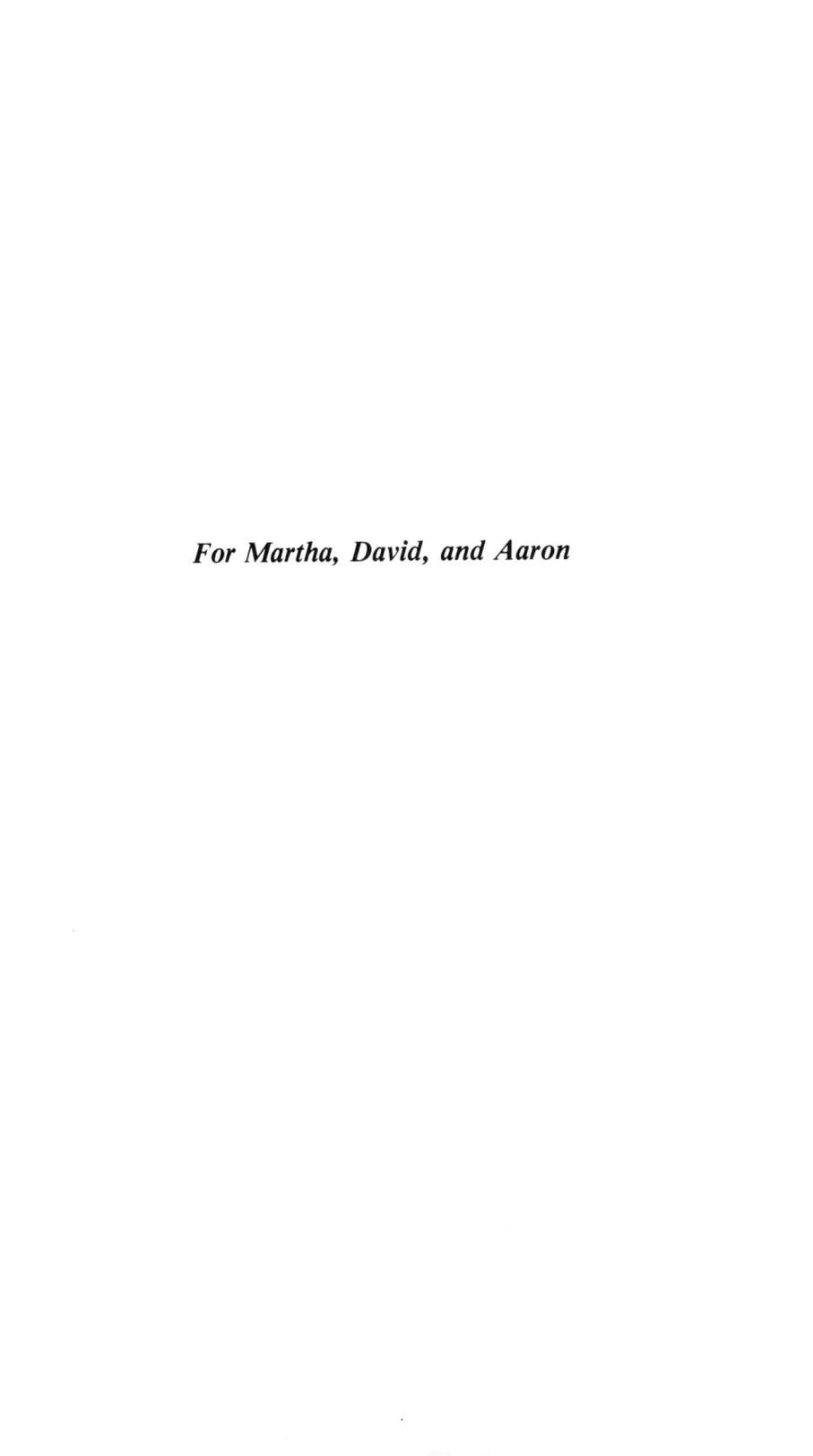

# Contents

|   | Preface | vii |
|---|---|---|
| 1. | Introduction: Of Questions and Problems | 1 |
| 2. | Franz Rosenzweig: From Philosophy to Religion<br>*"Biographical Absurda"*<br>*The Relationship Between Philosophy and Religion*<br>*The Critique of Philosophy*<br>*The Movement from Philosophy to Religion*<br>*The Religious Person's Life in the World* | 14 |
| 3. | Martin Buber: The Movement Toward Dialogue<br>*Mysticism and the Philosophy of Realization*<br>*The Philosophy of Dialogue*<br>*The Tensions within* I and Thou | 45 |
| 4. | Emil Fackenheim: The New "Vulnerability" to History<br>*Fackenheim's Early Theological Positions*<br>*The Confrontation with the Holocaust* | 87 |
| 5. | Conclusion: Wrestling with the Category of Revelation | 115 |
|   | Notes | 129 |
|   | Index | 150 |

# Preface

In the works of Rosenzweig, Buber, and Fackenheim we see struggles with the meaning of revelation which are based upon two assumptions, assumptions with which there is no widespread agreement today. The first assumption is that issues of Jewish belief are of importance for the present and future vitality of the Jewish community. The second is that the religious and philosophical insights that have been won by modern Jews in their effort to create a continuity with their past are relevant for religious people, and for people who take seriously religious issues, who do not belong to that particular community. At this time the majority of Jews, including significant numbers of Jewish leaders, teachers, and scholars believe that the affirmation of Jewish ethnicity and/or Jewish observance is sufficient to guarantee the present and future of the community. In addition, modern philosophers and theologians in other religious traditions have often completely ignored the endeavors of modern Jewish philosophers for the last two hundred years.

I agree with Rosenzweig, Buber, and Fackenheim that issues of modern Jewish belief are relevant to the vitality of the Jewish community and that the insights of modern Jewish thinkers are relevant to philosophers of religion and religious people outside of the Jewish community. I have tried to elucidate the powerful conceptions of these thinkers and also to point out some of the difficulties, both philosophical and for Jewish life, within these conceptions.

Rosenzweig and Buber affirmed that significant truth is only uncovered through a life with others. The views and conclusions that I have presented here have been deeply influenced by discussions with my colleagues in the department of Religion at Concordia University and with my students. My wife, Martha Saunders-Oppenheim, has helped me at all stages of this book, from the most theoretical to the most technical. I would like to thank Prof. Lawrence Kaplan of McGill University for a very sensitive and critical reading of an earlier version of this manuscript. I would also like to thank Concordia University for a grant that I received in connection with the publication of this book.

*Michael Oppenheim*
*Montreal, 1984*

# Chapter I
# Introduction: Of Questions and Problems

> *To ask a question is an act of the intellect; to face a problem is a situation involving the whole person. A question is the result of thirst for knowledge; a problem reflects a stance of perplexity, or even distress. A question calls for an answer, a problem calls for a solution.*
> Abraham Heschel[1]

> *Cognition no longer appears to me as an end in itself. It has turned into service, a service to human beings . . . Now I only inquire when I find myself inquired of. Inquired of, that is, by* men *rather than by scholars.*
> Franz Rosenzweig[2]

It is vital to recognize the distinction between questions and problems. Questions arise when the intellect finds itself at a momentary impasse. Although some questions have elicited heated controversy and serious efforts to find answers, the success or failure of the answers is of no consequence for everyday living. For example, it would be difficult to demonstrate that the efforts to answer such philosophical questions as the existence of other minds or the validity of the proofs of God's existence affect the ways in which people live with and relate to other human beings or to God. One might legitimately wonder whether people other than scholars would raise such questions.

## 2  What Does Revelation Mean for the Modern Jew?

Problems are much different than questions. Problems arise out of the lives of real individuals, people who have first and last names.[3] When a person is serious about living authentically in the world, he frequently comes upon urgent problems. Although problems clamour for solutions, these are usually not found quickly or simply. Rather, one struggles for a solution; and often the solution must be lived-out, that is, found and verified in the process of living day to day.

In the course of this book we will explore three problems, problems that coalesce around the relationship between man and God. Since these are true problems, in Heschel's sense, and not the questions of a "discipline," we will need to look into the lives of those who faced such problems. Three modern Jewish thinkers, Franz Rosenzweig, Martin Buber, and Emil Fackenheim each struggled with dimensions of the relationship between man and God. They were led to struggle with these problems, because they noted a tension between their philosophical standpoints and what was revealed to them about God through their interaction with the Jewish tradition, lives with other people, and experiences of God. The effort to achieve a harmony between their philosophical views and their experiences brought them to examine the relevance that belief in God's revelation holds for modern religious people.

The lives and thought of Rosenzweig, Buber, and Fackenheim exhibit dramatic movements that reflect their respective quests to find authentic affirmations of Jewish belief. The struggles of these men are personal and philosophical at the same time. These struggles delineate some of the most important religious dilemmas that face the modern Jew, as well as modern Western religious people of all traditions. Rosenzweig, Buber, and Fackenheim confronted the powerful challenges to religious belief that have arisen since the Enlightenment: the affirmation that man's autonomous reason is the only legitimate guide for living; the belief that God is no more than a product of man's inner life; the view that history is an affair in which only man and nature are participants. In rejecting these "idols" of enlightened Western man, these three Jewish philosophers came to give religious belief a foundation from which its ongoing battles with the present secular climate of opinion could be vigorously pursued. Rosenzweig asserted that only God's revelation to man could stand as the point of Archimedes for human authenticity. Buber held that the full human being is one who acknowledges and participates in the ongoing dialogue between man and man, and man and God. Fackenheim suggested that the religious person is cut off from God unless he has arrived at a committed openness to the possibility of God's radical intervention into present history.

In the forefront of Franz Rosenzweig's philosophical writings and personal reflections is the confrontation between a philosophical standpoint that asserts the inviolability of human reason and the standpoint of the man of faith who affirms that the relationship to God makes man fully human. He viewed philosophy and religion as competing ways of life. Philosophy represents the natural man's deepest and most heroic efforts to direct the self and give meaning to life. The philosopher holds that the isolated, autonomous person who heroically struggles with all of the elements of existence is the true human being. In contrast to these perennial claims of philosophy, Rosenzweig regarded the way of life offered by philosophy as fundamentally unreal and mistaken. He believed that there was an existential imperative for man to move from philosophy to religion, and his own life-history exhibits this movement. For Rosenzweig, the passage from philosophy to religion represents the rejection of a life of isolation and meaninglessness for one of communication and trust. Only the stance of faith in God as Creator, Revealer, and Redeemer binds man to existence in the deepest way and also provides guidance for his life. Rosenzweig's significance for modern religious people lies in the powerful way he depicted, in both writings and life-history, the conflict between and the passage from philosophy to religion.

The object of Martin Buber's struggles as well as the rhythm of his passage toward a solution differ greatly from those of Rosenzweig. During the first two decades of the twentieth century Buber labored to come to a genuine understanding of the possibility of real relationship between man and God. From his earliest years Buber was immune to the hold of a one-dimensional rationalism that dominated modern Jewish thought during the previous century. However, he was himself caught in romanticism, the intellectual and emotional reaction to rationalism. Thus, Buber did not suggest that God was merely a moral ideal; but under the influence of such eminent German mystics as Eckhart and Boehme, he understood God to be both impersonal and something that arose in the soul of man. In seeing God as nothing but a dimension or creation of man's inner life, Buber gave testimony to the essential autonomy of the creative individual. This individual had no need to encounter others, either God or other men, for he believed that the achievement of unity with ultimate reality lay within his powers as a solitary person. The eventual repudiation of this position and the affirmation of the life of dialogue with other men and with God marks the boundary between Buber's early and his mature thought. Buber's movement toward dialogue is both a development that reverberates in all his works and an important turning point in the religious thought of modern man.

The effort to sensitize his contemporaries to the possibility of God's radical intervention into present-day history permeates the later theological writings of Emil Fackenheim. Fackenheim's earlier work focused on two spheres of God's interaction with man: in the past God spoke and intervened in the life of the religious community on the plane of history, and in the present God addresses the individual in moments of insight and crisis. In presenting this understanding of the dimensions of the divine-human encounter Fackenheim was in fact in agreement with the basic stream of modern existentialist men of faith. However, he came to recognize the inadequacy of this position which resulted in effectively eliminating God's power over the present. He wrote that "the God of Israel cannot be God of either past or future unless He is still God of the present."[4] Fackenheim's passage from the safety of his earliest standpoints to his later "vulnerability" to history came as his response to the terror and challenge of the event of the Holocaust. The phrase "commanding voice of God in Auschwitz"[5] expresses his deepest attempts—extending over almost two decades—to find some fragmentary meaning in the Holocaust. His intense search to discover at least "hints or fragments which bespeak a meaning"[6] is of decisive import for all those who seek to affirm the reality of man's relationship with the God of the Bible.

In the above summaries of the philosophical and personal movements of Rosenzweig, Buber, and Fackenheim, it has repeatedly been claimed that these developments are of great significance for modern religious people. This claim rests on the relevance of the problems they addressed and the force of the solutions they found. While an analysis of their solutions will have to wait for the detailed treatments of the chapters that follow, the matter of the relevance of their problems can be explored at this time.

The problems that these three Jewish philosophers wrestled with have been prominent in Western thought from the period of the Enlightenment. Since the Enlightenment there have been many challenges to the religious man's belief that he lives in the presence of God. The radical questioning of that faith has, in the main, originated from two sources. First, the belief in God has been rejected because it came into conflict with *man's faith in himself,* even though those who have rejected such belief often have not bothered to engage in a serious debate about the reality of God. In repudiating all of the authorities of the past, Enlightenment man—and despite all the "crises" of Auschwitz, Hiroshima, and Vietnam, it is a mistake to underestimate the continued power of the premises of the Enlightenment —declared that he would not allow a Being to stand above him, who commands as well as judges. Second, the belief in God has been subjected to the onslaught of a seemingly invincible *psychological reductionism.*

Friedrich Nietzsche's declaration, "If God existed, how could I bear not to be God"[7] is the most forceful and famous statement that God must be rejected for the sake of man's autonomy. However, it was Hegel who earlier gave extensive philosophical utterance to this position. For Hegel philosophy is the standard-bearer of mankind's claims to autonomy. He affirmed that philosophy justifiably recognized as its own both the event and the content of revelation. He identified God or Absolute Spirit with the developing consciousness of man and held that this consciousness reached its ultimate climax in the self-understanding of the philosophic mind. Finally, Hegel abolished the biblical God from history by proposing that the philosopher's exposition of the necessary dialectical movement inherent in history expresses the same truth that is represented symbolically in the religious man's belief that God is the Lord of history. Belief in God's providence was to retain its place only in the minds of those who could not rise to the purer and clearer realm of philosophy.

The attack on religion that is placed under the rubric of "psychological reductionism" also has a history that goes back to the beginning of the Enlightenment. In David Hume's *The Natural History of Religion,* religious belief is seen to have its origin in the combination of fear and hope that primitive man felt in the face of a frightening and mysterious world. Yet, the full force of this critique of religious faith had to wait to be realized until Sigmund Freud's arrival on the scene. Freud, like the earlier philosophers of the Enlightenment, hoped that man had arrived at a stage of maturity that would allow him to release himself from everything and everyone that sought to keep him in the state of childhood and dependence. Freud believed that the time had arrived for mankind to set aside the illusion that there is a God and to reconcile itself to the truly difficult challenges of human autonomy. He sought to demonstrate that the belief in a personal God, in particular in a loving and caring Father, was nothing more than a fantasy created by the infantile wish for such a being. He asked man to recognize the illusory character of a divine being who acts in history. According to him, two of the major functions of such a being had become obsolete, namely the exorcism of the terrors of nature and the reconciliation of man to the cruelty of fate. Science did a fair job of the first and the mature person could face the latter on his own.[8]

While it is highly doubtful that the man in the street can identify the philosophers who gave expression to these critiques or can provide a fully formulated argument that incorporates the insights of such thinkers as Hume and Hegel, Nietzsche and Freud, there is no question but that at least in general these critiques have become the common stock of the majority in our society. The current climate of opinion has been significantly shaped by those philosophers who fought for what they saw as the legitimate rights of man against the illegitimate claims of an illusory God. It is in light of these philosophical and psychological challenges that we can recognize the relevance for modern religious man of the personal and philosophical struggles of our three modern Jewish thinkers. Rosenzweig protests against the pretext of human autonomy by affirming that only revelation provides true orientation for life. Buber responds to the age's apotheosis of man by asserting that man is fully human only when he participates in the dialogue with the "eternal Thou." Fackenheim overrides man's claim of complete control over history, a claim that is riddled with as much despair as confidence, by seeking to restore man's openness to the commanding voice of Him who speaks in the present.

We have briefly looked into the nature of Rosenzweig's, Buber's, and Fackenheim's efforts to meet the modern challenges to religion presented in the works of Hegel, Freud, and others. Before going on to the detailed treatments of the three modern Jewish philosophers, it is important to look into the question of what is *Jewish* in all of this discussion of challenges and responses to the problematics of modern religious belief.

The problems that these thinkers were compelled to address come from the environment they shared with Jews and non-Jews. Their earliest positions reflect this general environment more than the resources of the Jewish tradition itself. This is clearly the case in the appeal of philosophy to Rosenzweig, of romanticism to Buber, and of existentialism to Fackenheim. Yet, it is precisely the effort to confront those philosophical challenges that arise from outside the Jewish community that illuminates one of the ties that bind Rosenzweig, Buber, and Fackenheim to the stream of modern Jewish philosophy. The modern Jewish philosophical endeavor does not comprise a unity because of a fundamental agreement among its participants about the nature of Judaism or because of a tradition of thinkers who were strongly influenced by their predecessors

8   What Does Revelation Mean for the Modern Jew?

and sought either to develop or reject the systems or doctrines of those who preceded them. It is the struggle with some intense challenges of modernity, an identification with the Jewish experience, and a commitment to the present Jewish community that provides the stream of modern Jewish philosophy with a unity and integrity.[9]

As we have seen, their response to the multi-dimensional modern challenge to the past event and present reality of God's revelation to man binds together the thought of Rosenzweig, Buber, and Fackenheim. They believed that it was important for modern Jews to take seriously the challenges to religious belief, but they also held that an adequate response could be formulated, and that this response drew, in some significant ways, from the resources of the Jewish tradition. It was their identification with the Jewish experience, that is, the body of literature, values, and ways of life that have come together to form the ongoing Jewish tradition, that helped to mold their affirmation of God's revelation to man.

Rosenzweig's writings, for example, are permeated with elements from the yearly round of the Jewish liturgical experience. Both the prominence and the role of these elements reflect that religious experience in the synagogue during the Yom Kippur, Day of Atonement, service that dramatically transformed his life and thought in 1913. For Buber it was his complex dialogue with Hasidic literature, starting from 1904, and with the Hebrew Bible, that helped to crystallize his mature thought about the relationship between man and God. Fackenheim's interest in the literary genre of *midrash,* that Rabbinic mode of reply to historic catastrophe and to religious dilemma through story, helped to provide him with the means and the courage to struggle with the event of the Holocaust.

The lives of these three Jewish philosophers vividly demonstrate their dedication to the Jewish community of their times. In connection with Rosenzweig, his efforts to build up from nothing a dynamic program of adult education for German-Jews during the inter-war period is most note-worthy. Buber's contributions began with his early addresses on Judaism that were delivered in order to revive the power of Judaism in the lives of the youth of his generation. Throughout his life Buber's continual hope of giving an authentic Jewish spirit to the new movement of Zionism also brought him forward as a leader of tremendous dedication and importance. Fackenheim's struggles with the traumatic event of the Holocaust are one example of his leadership of the community. He is endeavoring to give direction and expression to the Jewish community's efforts to respond to the Holocaust, because he notes sparks of hope in the quiet and uneven response of this time.

While the encounter with the challenges of modernity, the commitment to the Jewish experience, and the dedication to the Jewish community are features that bind the work of Rosenzweig, Buber, and Fackenheim to the stream of modern Jewish philosophy, there is also a feature common to them that distinguishes them from many of their predecessors and contemporaries. These men rejected any and all varieties of rationalism, that rationalism that played so important a role in nineteenth century Jewish thought and which continued to influence many in the next century. Reason, both "pure" and "practical" is rejected as being either the essence of man or the foundation of the Jew's understanding of his religion. As part of the existentialist protest against rationalism, they seek to find the bases for the individual's self-understanding of himself as a human being and as a Jew in his experiences with God, his fellow man, and the world.

Rosenzweig continually proclaimed the inadequacies of reason alone to give man an understanding of the deepest elements in his life. Taking Hegel's "System" as the highest expression of man's attempt to grasp the world through the powers of reason, he proclaimed that Hegel's work had clearly failed to defend itself satisfactorily against the attacks of those who wished to know about the real world and not about just a possible, hypothetical world. Reason can only touch upon what is possible, according to Rosenzweig, and man thus must rely upon experience to tell him about himself and the universe. He rejected the liberal Judaism of his time as shallow for it identified Judaism with the ideals of practical reason. The basis of Judaism was seen by him in the historic covenant between God and the people of Israel at Sinai. Similarly, the individual Jew finds his own ties to the Jewish tradition in the fact or datum that he is born into the covenant with God. Rosenzweig begins his philosophy with man's experience of God, the world, and other men, and his understanding of the individual Jew takes as its starting point the facticity of the covenant and one's birth into that on-going relationship with God.

Throughout his work Buber acknowledged that reason could give man an orientation to the world of things, but he denied its power to speak of the more important dimensions of human life. Buber's early interest in mysticism was the outcome of his belief that man could come into contact with ultimate reality, in this case through mystical intuition. While Buber's philosophy of dialogue rejects his earlier mysticism, it is still motivated by his desire to go beyond the limits of reason. For Buber, the I-Thou relationship gives man a glimpse of the fullness of his world. Man encounters the full depth of the world about him, his fellow man, and the eternal God through this dialogue between "I" and "Thou." Buber's mature thought on Judaism also takes its basis in the ongoing dialogue between God and the people of Israel.

Emil Fackenheim's first essays attacked the use of religious idealism and religious naturalism by liberal North American Jewish thinkers in the fifth and sixth decades of the twentieth century. Fackenheim was not alone in this attack.[10] What distinguishes him from other Jewish theologians is the developments in his thought that followed this first position. Fackenheim at first founded his understanding of the nature of man and the individual's need for divine encounter on the universal dilemmas or contradictions of human life. He soon found, however, that this understanding did not stand firmly enough within the faith commitment and singled-out history of the Jewish community. The latest development in his thought, which begins in 1966 or 1967, reflects the impact of the challenge of the Holocaust. The events of the Holocaust and the establishment of the modern state of Israel brought him to examine the recent history of the community in search of fragmentary elements of God's commanding and redeeming voice.

Rosenzweig, Buber, and Fackenheim sought to forge authentic ways of being Jewish in the modern world. They shared the conviction that although the belief that man lives in the presence of God is under severe attack today, the living covenant between God and the Jewish people is the only genuine foundation for Jewish life. This relationship is not merely a symbol of some purely human reality for them. Yet, as thinkers who tried to meet the challenges of modernity rather than to ignore the world of today, they believed that a complete return to the faith of the fathers was not possible. In the solutions that Rosenzweig, Buber, and Fackenheim arrived at there are elements of doubt as well as elements of faith. A faith fully purged of doubt was for them as inauthentic as a way of life completely devoid of faith. The only possibility open to people of the present is a questioning faith, one that feels the power of Hegel, Nietzsche, and Freud, but is still able to respond forcefully. In the following pages we will explore the nature and dynamics of the particular responses of Rosenzweig, Buber, and Fackenheim. Since the problems that they faced are common to all modern religious people, the solutions that they arrived at and tested in their lives should be recognized as having a significance that extends beyond the boundaries of their religious community.

## Chapter II
# Franz Rosenzweig: From Philosophy to Religion

## I. "Biographical Absurda"

The conflict between philosophy and religion and the movement from the former as a way of life to the latter pervade the writings of Franz Rosenzweig. The first concern of this chapter is not to present a survey of Rosenzweig's writings, but to examine the events in Rosenzweig's life that both disclose the presence of this movement and demonstrate the bridge between his life and his thought. The importance of recognizing the bridge between life and thought was once underscored by Rosenzweig in a statement he made about the great nineteenth century religious figure, Soren Kierkegaard. Rosenzweig wrote that "behind each paradox of Kierkegaard one sees biographical *absurda,* and for this reason one must *credere.*"[1] Here Rosenzweig, in a brief allusion to Tertullian's maxim, gives expression to one of his most characteristic ideas: the verification of concepts takes place in the *life* of the thinker. One feels the truth of Kierkegaard's thoughts, because one knows that Kierkegaard did not just sit down to write fascinating pieces, but rather his thought was an outgrowth of the way in which he faced major crises in his life. Consequently, Rosenzweig is saying that to understand Kierkegaard's ideas one must be continually conscious of the important turning points in his life. Only in this way will the living issues behind some of Kierkegaard's more paradoxical philosophic stances not be lost.

Rosenzweig's statement about "biographical absurda" applies equally to himself. The central theme in Rosenzweig's writings, the movement from philosophy to religion—as well as such ancillary topics as the relationship between Judaism and Christianity and the imperative of revelation that directs one "into life"—all have such absurda as their foundation.

The major movements in Rosenzweig's life are dramatic and condensed into a few years. Rosenzweig undergoes two conversion experiences in the year 1913, the one *from philosophy* and the second a few months later *into Judaism*. By 1920, as evidenced by his letter to a former professor, Rosenzweig had formulated a basic orientation to the world and to other men that was to stand for the rest of his life. He wrote in this letter that in discovering his Judaism he had taken hold of his real self and now "cognition no longer appears to me as an end in itself. It has turned into service, a service to human beings."[2] From this time until his death in 1929 he devoted himself to a life of action, to a life of service.

Rosenzweig's early religious background was characteristic of middle-class, highly acculturated Jewish families in Germany in the second half of the nineteenth century.[3] He was educated in the German public schools and went to a gymnasium. He attended Hebrew school until he had learned Hebrew, and at the age of thirteen, in 1899, he had a *bar mitzvah*. His parents did not observe the Jewish Law, and went to the synagogue only on the most important religious holydays, *Rosh Hashana* and *Yom Kippur,* that is, New Year's Day and the Day of Atonement.

Rosenzweig's early indifference toward Judaism is indicated in some letters he wrote to his family in 1909.[4] Like many young Jews in Germany at this time, Rosenzweig believed that Judaism was an empty shell, something which one could inhabit out of custom or inertia, but certainly not out of any powerful convictions. Rosenzweig's contact with Judaism and with the Jews of his time and place brought him to conclude that the only significance of that religion was to be found in the registry office.

Between 1905 and 1913 Rosenzweig studied first medicine at the universities of Göttingen, Munich, and Freiburg, and later history and philosophy at Berlin and Freiburg. In Leipzig in early 1913 he began to speak with an old friend, Eugen Rosenstock, about philosophy, history, and religion. The meetings between these two, especially the meeting on the night of July 7, 1913, were to be decisive for Rosenzweig's religious development.[5]

Rosenstock, who had had only a very slight acquaintance with Judaism, had become a Christian; and his impassioned discussion showed the strength of Christianity in his life. Rosenstock later described that conversation as one

> concerned with questions of faith. But it was not Judaism and Christianity that were arrayed against each other, but rather faith based on revelation, (Offenbarungsglaube), was contrasted with faith in philosophy, (Philosophiegläubigkeit).[6]

Rosenzweig later confirmed this understanding of that night:

> In that night's conversation Rosenstock pushed me step by step out of the last relativist positions that I still occupied, and forced me to take an absolute standpoint. I was inferior to him from the outset, since I had to recognize for my part too the justice of his attack. If I could then have buttressed my dualism between revelation and the world with a metaphysical dualism between God and the Devil I should have been unassailable. But I was prevented from doing so by the first sentence of the Bible. This piece of common ground forced me to face him. This has remained even afterwards, in the weeks that followed, the fixed point of departure. Any form of philosophical relativism is now impossible to me.[7]

The first issue discussed that night was the conflict between philosophy and religion. Through his studies of Hegel and more recent philosophers such as Nietzsche, Rosenzweig had discovered the great difference between 1800 and 1900. The philosopher after Hegel could not speak of "objective truth" or of the System. Rosenzweig had found that only a philosophy that stressed personal decision and action could have validity in the twentieth century. He seems to have entered the discussion with Rosenstock from what might be called an existentialist position.[8] Rosenzweig held that philosophy must be integrated into the philosopher's life, and that the only perspective from which an individual could search for truth was his own experience and understanding. Rosenstock called this a relativist position, and countered that revelation offers a more fixed center for understanding the world. Revelation gives man a perspective that goes beyond the limits of his customary experiences and unaided understanding.

Rosenzweig's reference to creation in one of his letters quoted previously showed that he had already accepted the Biblical notion of the relationship between God and the world. Once Rosenzweig saw the implications of this understanding of creation, he found that the philosophic relativism of man on his own had to be rejected in favor of the binding character of God's revelation. Philosophic relativism was no longer possible for him, and he later made the category of revelation into the core of his religious thinking.

The conversation also had another stage. When Rosenzweig rejected his philosophic position, he was compelled to look into himself and to understand the meaning that Judaism had for his life. Rosenzweig, as he himself acknowledged, was forced to lay bare his own skeleton and to examine his own anatomy.[9]

In a letter of October 31, 1913, Rosenzweig wrote of this aspect of his meeting.[10] He said that he had been completely "disarmed" by Rosenstock's confession of faith. What surprised him was that Rosenstock, although both a very cultured person and a man who possessed a good historico-philosophical mind, had spoken out of the standpoint of Christian faith. Prior to that meeting, Rosenzweig did not believe that a thoroughly modern thinker, as Rosenstock was, could see himself as a religious man. Rosenzweig was surprised that Christianity still had the power and pathos to satisfy a man such as his friend. Rosenzweig's earlier contact with religion and religious men had left him unprepared for this meeting with Rosenstock. In seeing Rosenstock as a thoroughly religious man, whose

*Weltanschauung* and way of life were so self-consciously Christian, Rosenzweig began to reflect upon his own experience of the lifeless Judaism he had known.

As a letter of late 1913 indicates, Rosenzweig later came to recognize the truth of Rosenstock's position and formulated his own version of it.[11] He took up Schelling's idea that the modern age was "the Johannine period." He saw that Christianity had always worked in the world, transforming the natural matter of creation into spirit by extending God's work of revelation throughout the world. The Johannine period was the final chapter in this process. It had been inaugurated when the word of revelation finally overcame philosophy's continual opposition to any source of truth beyond the natural mind. Hegel's philosophical-theological system was the beginning point. Now the "Word" of revelation that Christianity carried had no opposition and could forcefully include all men and all of life in its "body."

Reflecting upon these discoveries, Rosenzweig began to "reconstruct" his world. However, it is obvious that this new view still meant that there was "no room for Judaism." Judaism had begun the process of bringing God's revelation to the world, but once Christianity entered the scene, Judaism became anachronistic. Jewish life had neither any intensity nor any meaning for the modern man, as far as Rosenzweig could see. At this time he decided to become a Christian, but his historical sensitivity compelled him to first learn a little more about Judaism. Even if he was not a Christian, he was still not a "pagan." Rather than enter the Church as an uncircumcised pagan, Rosenzweig wanted to acknowledge his Jewish background and to re-traverse the road of the earliest Christians. This personal "reservation" was the beginning of his more serious relationship to Judaism.

In the coming months and years Rosenzweig changed some of the ideas that he expressed here. However, there are aspects of this immensely important dialogue that Rosenzweig carried with him the rest of his life. First, Rosenzweig never brought himself to question the validity of Christianity both as one of the true paths to God and as a living reality in the life of modern man.

One might expect that when Rosenzweig turned from Christianity to affirm Judaism he would augment his rejection of Christianity by rather polemic thrusts. It certainly is not unusual for someone to violently attack that which he first found to be the "truth" for him. Rosenzweig did not do this, and his deep experiences with Rosenstock were the reason. Rosenzweig found that at least one man whom he knew to be thoroughly upright and sincere had discovered in *Christianity* a pathway to God, and Rosenzweig could henceforth never deny this reality. In addition, his respect for Rosenstock as a thinker and a full man of his time brought him to understand that Christianity had a real role in the modern world. Whatever might change in the future, Rosenzweig now had vivid experiences that forever lay at the foundation of his thinking about religion.

Second, it was from such conversations as this one with his friend that Rosenzweig learned of the power of dialogue. In later years Rosenzweig could speak of the immense possibilities of a meeting between people, when both stand facing one another with trust and openness, because he had experienced all of this with Rosenstock. In fact, one can trace the major turning points of Rosenzweig's life to such dialogues, dialogues with men and with God. In light of the multi-faceted ramifications of this single encounter, the significance of both "biographical absurda" and the power of dialogue in Rosenzweig's life-history could not be more evident.

Rosenzweig returned to his home in Cassel after the discussion with Rosenstock, and he attended the Jewish New Year's service in the synagogue of his family on October 2 and 3. Afterward, he told his parents of his plans to attend the service for the Day of Atonement in preparation for his movement into the Church. His mother was angry at this disclosure, and refused to allow him to enter the synagogue again. Rosenzweig then traveled to Berlin where he prayed in a small orthodox synagogue on October 11.[12] It was in this new environment that Rosenzweig came to a breakthrough in his view of Judaism. There must have been something in these new pious surroundings that he had never found in his family's usual place of worship.

The experience of that Yom Kippur, which is the most important day of the Jewish calendar, left an indelible mark on Rosenzweig. Although he never speaks of that experience in his letters or books, one can gain a sense of what he felt that day from his quite passionate description of the Yom Kippur service in *The Star of Redemption*.[13] Rosenzweig writes in the *Star* that only on this day does the Jew kneel, and he does not kneel in confession or in pleading for forgiveness, but "in beholding the immediate nearness of God."[14] As a "single band" the congregation "prostrates itself before the King of Kings," and "anticipates the moment of eternal redemption by seizing on it now, in the present."[15] All of this is expressed not in words, but in the graphic gesture of kneeling:

> God lifts up his countenance to the united and lonely pleading of men . . . Man's soul is alone—with God . . . In this moment man is as close to God . . . as it is ever accorded him to be.[16]

On October 23, Rosenzweig gives the first indication of his radical shift toward Judaism. In a letter to his mother, he writes that the " 'connection of the innermost heart with God' which the heathen can only reach through Jesus is something the Jew already possesses."[17]

This letter marks the end of three to four months of self-examination for Rosenzweig. The conversation with Rosenstock, in July, 1913, convinced him that God's word could never be irrelevant for man. He was led to see that the philosopher's attempt to look at the world from the point of view of man's understanding alone had to be supplemented by an encounter with God's revelation. Rosenzweig saw his own life as a movement from faith in philosophy to religious faith. Even while he was still learning about the nature of religious faith, Rosenzweig recognized that the movement from philosophy was irreversible.

The conversion experience of October brought much in its wake. Of primary importance is Rosenzweig's certainty that God *does* speak to the Jew through the community's liturgy. He once said that Yom Kippur is "a testimony to the reality of God which cannot be controverted."[18] This point cannot be over-emphasized. In his latter works Rosenzweig nowhere even endeavors to argue for his belief that God still speaks to the Jewish community. *He* had experienced God's voice, and thus he knew that the Voice was there to be heard. In addition, Rosenzweig never put aside his new awareness of the importance of the calendar and liturgy in the religious life of man. He continued to maintain that for both the Jew and the Christian the liturgical dimension of the community's experience introduces the "eternal" into daily life. Finally, not questioning his previous belief that Christianity played a vital role in God's redemption of the world, he now eagerly sought to uncover Judaism's role in this plan.

In that same eventful year Rosenzweig began the long process of "making clear to myself the entire system of Jewish doctrine."[19] He became a student of Professor Hermann Cohen, who had left the University of Marburg to teach Jewish philosophy at the *Lehranstalt für die Wissenschaft des Judentums* in Berlin. In April, 1914, Rosenzweig attempted to formulate his ideas on religion. His essay "Atheistic Theology"[20] takes as its point of departure his criticism of some modern trends in theology which either dilute or ignore the concept of revelation. Rosenzweig's studies and thinking continued during the next four years, while he was in the Red Cross and the army.

From the end of May, 1916, to December of the same year, Rosenzweig and Rosenstock had a most important exchange of letters. The extensive correspondence of these few months was a passionate continuation of their discussions of July, 1913. However, there was also a striking difference between the two "meetings." Rosenzweig no longer saw himself as a philosopher who stood opposed to the man of faith. Now there was a sometimes heated exchange of views between Rosenzweig's developing Jewish self-understanding and Rosenstock's powerful Christianity.

The correspondence had a profound effect upon Rosenzweig's thinking, especially in terms of his understanding of revelation. At one point Rosenzweig asked Rosenstock to explain his understanding of the "relation between Nature and Revelation."[21] Rosenstock's answer was that revelation brings orientation. After revelation there exists a real Above and Below in the world, and a real Before and After in time.[22] Prior to being touched by God's word, the natural man takes his own position in the world as the locus of points. Where he stands is the middle of the earth, and his birth is the proper beginning point in time. However, this relativism is overcome by God's revelation. Revelation gives man a standard beyond himself. He begins to see his life in terms of God's plan and he enters into the stream of life assured of an unchanging position from which to view the world. In a letter to Rudolf Ehrenburg in October, 1917, Rosenzweig speaks of Rosenstock's answer, that "revelation is orientation" (*Offenbarung ist Orientierung*), as presenting him with the "point of Archimedes" (*Archimedespunkt*) for his own thinking.[23]

Rosenzweig began writing *The Star of Redemption* on August 22, 1918, while fighting on the Balkan front, and he finished it in February, 1919. While a complete analysis of the *Star* will not be attempted here, it will help in understanding Rosenzweig's life to have a general grasp of the structure and line of argument of this book. The structure of the *Star* parallels Rosenzweig's philosophic and religious growth. The first part examines Idealism and the existentialist philosophers who followed in the wake of Hegel. The second part describes the new orientation to God, the world, and man that crystallizes with the sudden religious experience of God's revelation. The third part illustrates how the religious man's new understanding of himself directs him into the world as both a member of a community of believers and a man given a specific task by God in the ongoing redemption of the world. The *Star* describes the movement from the philosopher to the religious man and religious actor in the world.

Rosenzweig saw the *Star* as more than a system of philosophy. It was intimately tied to his life, "as a pledge for the future, as well as a hieroglyphic of the past and present."[24] The *Star* allowed Rosenzweig to rethink his past development. He was able to see the limits of philosophy and the necessity that it be augmented by religion. The *Star* takes its place as an effort of Rosenzweig to gain insight into his own movement from philosopher to religious man. In addition, Rosenzweig was able to reaffirm his existence as a Jew, combining the fruits of his study of early Jewish sources, of Hebrew, and Jewish Law, with his understanding of Judaism's role in the modern world.

As a "pledge for the future," the *Star* disclosed those areas of study, especially Jewish Law, that needed to be given more attention. It also pointed to Rosenzweig's future work within the Jewish community. In a foreword to the second edition of the *Star* in 1925, Rosenzweig wrote that the "reconciliation" of the book can only come with ending it. He held that philosophizing should be done just once and that "the book is not an end in itself." It needs justification which is found in life's days. Thus, the book "leads into life."[25]

A letter of 1920 to Friedrich Meinecke, one of Rosenzweig's former professors, represents an autobiographical recapitulation of the ground that he had traversed and a signpost to direct him into the future. The letter followed the publication of his doctoral dissertation, *Hegel and the State*. A clear road to an academic position had consequently been opened up. However, he rejected this path, and decided to devote all of his time to Judaism and especially to the vital and perplexing problem of Jewish education. Rosenzweig had, a few months earlier, tried to explain why he was refusing Meinecke's offer of a university lectureship, but he felt that his reasons still remained obscure. In trying to explain his position on this question, he gives a new perspective to his religious development since 1913:

> In 1913 something happened to me for which *collapse* is the only fitting name. I suddenly found myself on a heap of wreckage, or rather I realized that the road I was then pursuing was flanked by unrealities. Yet this was the very road defined for me by my talent, and my talent only! . . . I felt a horror of myself . . . Amidst the shreds of my talents I began to search for my self, amidst the manifold for the One. It was then . . . that I descended into the vaults of my being, to a place whither talents could not follow me; that I approached the ancient chest whose existence I have never wholly forgotten, for I was in the habit of going down at certain times of the year to examine what lay uppermost in the chest: those moments had

all along been the supreme moments of my life . . . [This time, however, my hands dug deeper, bringing up armfuls of treasures.] These, indeed, were my own treasures, my most personal possessions, things inherited, not borrowed! By owning them and ruling over them I had gained something entirely new, namely the right to live—and even to have talents; for now it was *I* who had the talents, not they who had me.

. . . I had turned from a historian (perfectly "eligible" for a university lectureship) into an (utterly "ineligible") philosopher. The one thing I wish to make clear is that scholarship no longer holds the center of my attention, and that my life has fallen under the rule of a "dark drive" which I'm aware that I merely *name* by calling it "my Judaism" . . . Cognition no longer appears to me as an end in itself. It has turned into service, a service to human beings . . . Now I only inquire when I find myself *inquired of.* Inquired of, that is, by *men* rather than by scholars. There is a man in each scholar, a man who inquires and stands in need of answers. I am anxious to answer the scholar *qua* man but not the representative of a certain discipline, that insatiable, ever inquisitive phantom which like a vampire drains him whom it possesses of his humanity. I hate that phantom as I do all phantoms. Its questions are meaningless to me. On the other hand, the questions asked by human beings have become increasingly important to me. This is precisely what I mean by "cognition and knowledge as a service:" a readiness to confront such questions, to answer them as best I can out of my limited knowledge and my even slighter ability.[26]

The first part of this letter describes Rosenzweig's attempt, coming out of a deep sense of depression and emptiness in 1913, to discover who he was and how he should orient his life. This letter may at first seem to conflict with the portrait given previously of Rosenzweig's religious development, in which the movement to Judaism came only after the pivotal conversation with Rosenstock and his interest in Christianity. In this letter to Meinecke, Rosenzweig suggests that in 1913 he had lost hold of his self and that in taking his Judaism as something central and not peripheral he began to feel in control. Although this letter does not mention Rosenstock or Christianity—and this may be because of the person for whom the letter was intended—it supplements rather than conflicts with the previous portrait. The letter to Meinecke discloses Rosenzweig's later reflections—it is seven years after his "return" to Judaism—upon his development. He now understands that the progress from his early indifference to Judaism to his eventual commitment is the major theme of his life. In comparing the two views of Rosenzweig's religious maturation, what comes to light is that he, like many other sensitive people, revises his understanding of his past in order to assimilate his experience and standpoint in the present.

The second part of the letter indicates that the academic world was rejected not only as a consequence of Rosenzweig's dedication to Judaism, but because he found the academic life to be empty. He believed that the academic world was filled with phantoms. Questions were asked but no real men were asking them. There was no contact between these voiceless queries and the problems of people living in the world. In contrast to that situation, Rosenzweig now found that as headmaster of the *Lehrhaus,* an institution of Jewish adult education, he was in touch with the questions that arose from people's struggles with themselves and the world. Cognition and knowledge were henceforth put into a more authentic relationship with life. Life did not serve cognition, but rather, cognition served life.

This letter clearly illustrates Rosenzweig's understanding of himself in his development from academic philosopher or historian to his life as religious man and educator. Although he described his present status as that of a philosopher, a little reflection will reveal that Rosenzweig was speaking of a special type of philosopher. Rosenzweig was certainly not describing the philosopher who belongs to one or another philosophical school, or one who lived for his writings. Rosenzweig saw in himself the combination of religious man and philosopher. He was a "philosopher" who would no longer write books, who would rather live as the principal of a struggling adult education school than take a solid position in an academic chair. Since he was a special type of "philosopher," who rejected academic life and committed himself to his community's struggle for meaning and existence, he was truly ineligible for an academic position.

The type of person that one usually thinks of as a philosopher, that type of person that Rosenzweig often attacked in his writings, would be suitable for such a position in just the same ways that Rosenzweig now was—and desired to be—ineligible.

From the time that Rosenzweig stopped going to school and entered the army, he concerned himself with the survival of the Jewish community in the face of the day-to-day threats of assimilation and secularization. This life of service had two major foci: commitment to Jewish education and translation of the past sources of Judaism. His writings on education laid the foundation for a school of adult education, the *Freies Jüdisches Lehrhaus,* that was established in Franfort in 1920. Rosenzweig was appointed the first head of the *Lehrhaus* in that year and he held that post until 1922, when he resigned because of the progressive paralysis he suffered due to lateral sclerosis.

One of the tasks that occupied Rosenzweig during his last years was the effort to make the past sources of Judaism come alive for his generation. Beginning in 1922 and continuing until its publication in 1924, Rosenzweig worked on the translation, with extensive commentary, of the poems of the famous medieval Jewish poet-philosopher Jehudah Halevi.[27] His other major effort at translation, in collaboration with Martin Buber, consisted in a new German translation of the Hebrew Bible. The joint work began in the spring of 1925 and continued until Rosenzweig's death in 1929.

Rosenzweig's intellectual development somehow was not denied in spite of all these practical matters and what he had called the demands of the day. Two projects in particular require some illumination. First, in 1921, at a publisher's invitation, Rosenzweig began working on a small manuscript titled *On Understanding the Sick and the Healthy.*[28] This work was to be a popularized account of the very difficult themes in the *Star.* Most of its material was taken from Rosenzweig's lectures at the *Lehrhaus.*

*On Understanding the Sick and the Healthy* dramatically presents Rosenzweig's belief that there is an existential necessity that underlies the individual's movement from philosophy to religion, or into life. The book contrasts common sense or the "healthy understanding" with philosophy, or what is called the "sick understanding." The term "common sense" is somewhat misleading if one takes it without clarification.[29] Rosenzweig means by it that way of living in the world which accepts the three bases of human life: God, the world, and other men. Thus, Rosenzweig holds that the belief in God is not something that only a few odd people maintain, but that it is so much a foundation for life that it is an essential part of man's "common sense."

Second, when in 1925 a new edition of *The Star of Redemption* was released, Rosenzweig included along with it an essay, "The New Thinking."[30] This essay appropriately stands as a supplement to the *Star* and as a further development of some of Rosenzweig's most characteristic thoughts. Just as the *Star* rests on some unique events in Rosenzweig's life-history, the essay takes its spirit from the same source. Rosenzweig's attack on philosophy's abstract disposition is followed by a portrayal of what "the new thinking" or the new philosophy should be like. The abstract is replaced by the most concrete kind of thinking, itself characterized by taking both time and other people seriously. The philosopher who sits alone meditating at his desk is similarly contrasted to the living thinker who learns about himself and the world through encounters. One can vividly see Rosenzweig's past meetings with Rosenstock and his unending flow of letters to many different people behind these statements.

All of Rosenzweig's work from 1922 to 1929 came against the backdrop of his paralyzing sickness, lateral sclerosis. Although the diagnosis in 1922 included the prognosis that the patient had no more than a year to live, Rosenzweig continued to think and write, with the aid of his wife, until his death on December 10, 1929.

## II. The Relationship Between Philosophy and Religion

Franz Rosenzweig's description of the multifaceted relationship between philosophy and religion is the focus of the second section of this chapter. Three themes disclose the nature of this relationship: the critique of philosophy, the movement from philosophy to religion, the religious person's life in the world. The spearhead of the critique of philosophy is Rosenzweig's portrait of the individual's life in the world. This portrait sets up the opposition between philosophy's abstract, deterministic image of man and the real living man who experiences the concreteness, finitude, and contingency of existence. The second theme, the movement from philosophy to religion, has its setting in the inner life of man. God's revelation transforms the individual from an isolated self to an enlightened soul. Finally, Rosenzweig's description of the religious person's life in the world underscores the religious man's turning to others. In response to God's call, the individual is thrust into the human world in the deepest way.

## The Critique of Philosophy

Rosenzweig looked upon philosophy as an integrated whole. In particular, he believed that there was a single line of development that wove itself through the whole history of philosophy. Philosophy originated with the pre-Socratics of Iona and culminated two thousand years later in Jena, where Hegel philosophized. For Rosenzweig philosophy was synonymous with Idealistic Philosophy and Hegel was understood as the last stage in the process. The drastic criticism of this discipline is aimed expressly at Hegel. Hegel embodied, in its highest form, the perennial effort of reason to give a systematic, that is, a complete, abstract, logical description of reality.[31]

The unity of philosophy is also understood from the point of view of its perennial presuppositions and inclinations. Rosenzweig held that philosophy has its foundation in the presupposition that reason provides the highest source of insight into the ultimate truths about man, the world, and God. Philosophy assumes that through the sustained, critical use of reason man can construct a system that is an accurate, coherent reflection of reality. These presuppositions about human reason and the possibility of being able to systematize reality leads philosophy to identify thought with being. It is held not only that reason has the capacity to penetrate all corners of the universe, but, in addition, that the structure and processes of thought are identical with the structure and processes that underlie the world. Those disciplines that illustrate the processes of the mind and are its most secure products, that is, logic and mathematics, are taken as valid models of the world itself. These idealistic characteristics of philosophy never vary, whether in Iona or Jena.

In reacting against philosophy and especially Hegel, Rosenzweig emphasized those features of man's life in the world that philosophy had ignored. In particular, he noted philosophy's failure to recognize: the singularity or uniqueness of the individual, the experience of living in time, the life of freedom and decision, the role of human passions, and the absolute distinction between man and God.

In *The Star of Redemption* Rosenzweig held that philosophy denied the reality of the individual. It sought to rid the world of all that was singular, and it thus collapsed the distinction between "the being of man and the being of the world."[32] Human existence shriveled away as the higher perspective that sought the "all of cognition" prevailed. In addition, philosophy's misappropriation of ethics further strengthened its inclination to deny the uniqueness of the individual. Although modern German Idealism had in fact spoken of ethics, the individual's ethical life had actually been dismissed. Philosophy saw the single man's life as nothing more than a petty example of what is incorporated into the ethical law. For the philosopher, ethics was not related to the single man, since its "true" character only came out in the universal ethical law or the laws of the State.[33]

In reaction to philosophy's misappropriation of the ethical, Rosenzweig described his new view of man as "metaethical" (*das Metaethische*).[34] The core of this understanding is the "singular life of the singular person."[35] Every individual sees himself as a member of the species, but at a deeper level he is conscious of his separateness or singularity. This aspect of the individual's self-consciousness derives from the uniqueness of his character. In the character of each man one has an example of man's being, or his "being there" in the world, which is prior to all thought. The individual discovers that he is self-contained and that with his particular character he stands in opposition to the world. He refuses to be totally assimilated into the world or to be reduced to some common essence by thought, because he defiantly affirms that in the particularity of his being lies all he means by his "self." The singularity of the individual's character cannot be absorbed into a common classification, and thus the individual stands alone in the world. Rosenzweig writes:

> Precisely this is his essence: that he will not be tapped into bottles; that he is eternally "still there;" that he ever exalts over the peremptory dictate of the universal in his distinctiveness; that for him his own distinctiveness is . . . his essence.[36]

The individual's consciousness of living in time is another important dimension of man's life in the world which philosophy had ignored. According to Rosenzweig, the "old thinking" of "philosophy is timeless and wants to be timeless."[37] This feature of philosophy is a consequence of its concerns to be systematic and to uncover the "essence" of things. In endeavoring to contain man and the world in a system, philosophy had proclaimed that unaltered "being" must be the background for grasping all things. Philosophy banned time, that is, the reality of things changing and developing over time, because this would undermine the tight parameters of the system. The quest for essences also required that any notion of change or movement in time be dismissed, since so-called essences do not change over time. Rosenzweig held that although common sense knows that the world cannot be understood outside of the flow of time, "the philosopher . . . retreats from the flow of reality into . . . the region of essences."[38]

Despite philosophy's protestations, Rosenzweig saw that the individual in existence could only be understood against the background of the flux of time. Man experiences time as an unceasing flux or stream. Everything is in process, because temporal things know no halts, no points of rest, outside of death itself. Rosenzweig's understanding of time is best given in his description of the moment in the *Star*. The individual's experience of a continual succession of moments ultimately leads to the realization that there is no fixed point within time. Even the concept of the present or the moment is no more than a fictional or, as it were, mathematical point within this succession. The moment is forever disappearing, being devoured by the past. It disappears before it can be grasped, and thus man experiences flux rather than any significant present time.[39] Rosenzweig concluded that "becoming" rather than "being" is the background against which man and the world must be understood.

Rosenzweig's critique of philosophy includes the conviction that philosophy eliminated freedom and decision from its description of human existence. The identification of thought and being resulted in this disregard of the life of freedom and decision. Rosenzweig wrote that when existence is interpreted in terms of logos, life is denied its liveliness.[40] In transferring the laws of logic to the world, philosophy abolished the concept of freedom from its study. Every event or action was interpreted as a necessary consequence of its antecedent conditions. What the individual had at one time experienced in terms of his freedom, now was explained as necessary.

Rosenzweig's most important statements about the life of freedom and decision are made in the context of discussions about the development of the individual and the significance of "meetings" in this development. He proclaimed that a person only becomes fully human through encounters with God, the world, and other people. Although one can thus generalize about the impact of such meetings, the meetings themselves are unique. In particular, Rosenzweig's recognition that human existence is permeated by freedom was derived from his understanding of the dynamics of the life of dialogue. The spontaneity and surprise that is often manifest in dialogue, and the recollection of how he and others had been truly transformed by these events, gave Rosenzweig incontestable experience of human freedom. Thus, in opposition to philosophy's declaration that the laws of logic take precedence over the individual's consciousness of his freedom, Rosenzweig upheld the common sense view that acknowledges the reality of man's freedom to hear and act.

The critique of philosophy's portrait of man included an examination of the role of passions in human life. Rosenzweig suggested that the individual had become "translated into mental terms"[41] by philosophy, that is, transformed into pure mind. Philosophy eradicated the life of passions by identifying man with the cognitive I or Ego. It contended that cognition was the most prominent element in human life and that speculation was man's most humane activity.

The existing individual's life of passion provides Rosenzweig with a key to a genuine understanding of man and the world. In the *Star* the insights afforded by the individual's fear of death and experience of love are the core of Rosenzweig's "system of philosophy."[42] These passions undermine philosophy's cognitively-derived picture of reality, re-orienting the individual to another, truer world.

In the beginning of the *Star,* for example, Rosenzweig utilizes man's fear of death to demonstrate one dimension of philosophy's failure to understand human existence. This book opens with the statement, "From death, from the fear of death, arises all cognition of the All."[43] The fear that death will someday swallow up the individual and all of his creations brings him to look to philosophy for some answer to the problem of death. Philosophy has always offered the same formula to alleviate the problem of death. It relates that the essential I is identical with God and the world, and thus that death is only an illusion. However, Rosenzweig suggests that the sting of death still remains, since the individual does not want to know about his "essence," but about *himself* in the only way that matters, as a distinct individual of body and soul. Thus, Rosenzweig uses man's very real fear of death and philosophy's failure to provide any comfort as the principle wedge to destroy "the System."

Philosophy's understanding of God brings forward the final component of Rosenzweig's critique. Rosenzweig recognized a general pantheistic tendency in philosophy. When thought was taken as the highest principle, God was transformed into just another manifestation of thought. This tendency of philosophy found its culmination in modern German Idealism, when the being of God was included in the absolute Ego of man.

One consequence of this reductionism was that God's relationship to man, and especially God's revelation, was reinterpreted. Revelation was no longer conceived of as a meeting or dialogue between two subjects, because man was both the only real subject and the only real object in the universe. Revelation, especially for Hegel, became something immanent in man's history. It was reinterpreted as a moment or series of moments in mankind's progressive understanding of the nature of the self. Thus, even where the terms "God" and "revelation" remained, philosophy denied the existence of any being that transcended the human sphere.

In the *Star* Rosenzweig attacked both the underlying pantheism of modern philosophy and the "reductive method" that characterizes the whole history of this discipline. Philosophy insists on positing one element—either God, the world, or man—as the reality that stands behind the other two.[44] In contrast to this general method of philosophy and its particular expression in modern times, Rosenzweig affirmed that God, the world, and man are not different than they appear to the individual in his concrete experiences of them. He introduced the "and" of separate existence in place of philosophy's use of the copula "is," i.e., "God (in reality) *is* X." The existence of God *and* the world *and* man is the foundation of Rosenzweig's philosophy of meeting. Man can know about God, the world and other men because he finds himself brought face to face with them in his living in the world. The *Star* is Rosenzweig's attempt to build a system upon those experiences in which the gulf between God, the world and man is spanned. He writes in the essay "The New Thinking,"

> To have cognition of God, the world, and man is to know what they do or what is done to them in these tenses of reality, and to know what they do to one another or what is done to them by one another. And here we presuppose that these three have separate existence, for if they were not separate, they could not act upon one another ... God, man, and the world

reveal themselves only in their relations to one another, that is, in creation, revelation, and redemption . . .[45]

Thus, Rosenzweig's sharp critique of philosophy takes its point of departure from a profound understanding of the individual's life in the world. The proof that philosophy allows the real man to elude its grasp is revealed through its failure to take such fundamental dimensions of human life into consideration as; the singularity of the individual, the experience of living in time, the life of freedom and decision, the role of human passions, and the absolute distinction between man and God.

## ADDENDUM: The "Point of View" Philosopher (*Der Standpunktsphilosoph*)[46]

Rosenzweig's treatment of philosophy also included those modern philosophers who, like himself, rejected systematic philosophy. Such modern philosophers as Kierkegaard, Schopenhauer, and especially Nietzsche represented all thinkers who search for authenticity in existence by taking the unabstracted man of body and soul as their foundation. Although Rosenzweig was very sympathetic to this new "point of view" philosophy, he also saw that a great difficulty presented itself when the new point of departure was "the subjective, the extremely personal self."[47] He questioned whether the insights of these philosophers could have any meaning or validity for someone other than the particular man whose experiences lay at its foundation.

Despite the reform that the "point of view" philosophers provided, Rosenzweig still thought of them within the context of those who, beginning in ancient Greece, tried to understand the world by means of human faculties alone. The limitations and also the heroism of philosophers, and Nietzsche in particular, were explored by Rosenzweig by looking at the figure of the tragic hero as he appeared in the classical Greek tragedy. Rosenzweig held that the tragic hero embodied the way of life of all natural men. The hero endeavored to live authentically in the world, but he showed a major defect in that he could not go outside of himself to live in dialogue with God and with other men. The tragic hero's solitary battle is against death. Mistrusting the world, and alone with himself, "death, his own death, has become the sovereign event of his life."[48]

In view of Rosenzweig's understanding of the natural man who is locked within himself, he held that it was inevitable that the new philosopher's ideas could not be communicated to and appropriated by other men. The only thing such men share in common is their fear of death, but this *angst* merely accentuates the absolute isolation of each man. According to Rosenzweig, one cannot found a philosophy that stresses the meaningfulness of dialogue between men on the individual's fear of death.[49] Thus, the modern philosopher who speaks out of his particular experiences and looks upon a world where he stands at its center, is still limited by the defects of the natural man. Rosenzweig saw Nietzsche's philosophy of idiosyncratic aphorisms as the logical culmination of all these factors.

## The Movement from Philosophy to Religion

The movement from philosophy to religion, from the tragic hero to the man who lives in God's presence, occurs when God turns to man. Rosenzweig held that God's turning, his revelation to man, was the "Archimedes point" of all of his thinking.[50] Taking an insight which came from one of Rosenstock's letters of 1916,[51] Rosenzweig explained how revelation transforms man, by using the word "orientation."[52] Revelation allows man to encounter the world in a new way. The world is neither alien nor fraught with danger, but the stage upon which man meets and works with God and with other men. The way in which revelation brings orientation will become clear in the process of analyzing Rosenzweig's understanding of God's turning toward man.

There are two basic aspects of the word *revelation* as it is found in Rosenzweig's word.[53] Revelation is first a public event in the past, and second, a personal experience in the present. As an event in history, God's two revelations form the basis for the two religious communities, the Jewish community and the

Christian community. At particular points in the past God revealed himself to assemblies of people. Those who belonged or later became part of one or the other of these assemblies found that the world had been placed in a new context. The religious community understands the point of time of God's covenant as the beginning of a new order which is the focal point of all history. The event brings with it a permanent sense of before and after. The fact that for much of the world history is separated into B.C. and A.D. indicates how God's revelation orders all of time. If the public event provides man with a common point of reference in the past, it also colors the way in which the future is conceived. Those within the religious community not only share conceptions of what constitutes their past, but specific hopes and expectations about the future are similarly held in common. God's revelation, which introduces the eternal into the temporal, thus provides the religious man with a scheme or pattern. All of time revolves around the one point in the past and the anticipated event in the future.

Revelation is meaningful to modern man, Rosenzweig held, because it is experienced in the present. In this way the present is tied to the past, and the individual becomes part of the community. Rosenzweig wrote:

> The ground of revelation is midpoint and beginning in one; it is revelation of the divine name. The constituted congregation and the composed world live their lives from the revealed name of God up to the present day, up to the present moment, and into the personal experience.[54]

The personal dimension of revelation, in addition to binding the individual to the community's historical experiences, traditions, and perceptions of the world, gives him a sense of the meaningfulness of his particular life. It is not enough that one is given general outlines of world history, one must feel that he has a significant part to play within this history. The religious man believes that he has a particular task. He finds himself, in all of his individuality and distinctiveness, addressed by God and asked to act in the world. He trusts that in the process of living he will discover what must be done.[55]

In the view of Rosenzweig's understanding of revelation, the continuity between creaturely existence and the religious life is maintained. By speaking of revelation as orientation, Rosenzweig can describe the real change that God's meeting with man effects, without implying that man must discard his past. Man builds his new understanding upon his own past experiences and perspectives. The religious man believes that he has a fuller understanding of the world. He realizes that as an isolated individual he was confronted by a world which he was not yet ready to openly meet. The individual who has experienced God's word and God's care finds himself in a new situation. He is compelled to turn towards others, and to aid God in working for the world's redemption.

The movement from isolated self to enlightened soul was portrayed by Rosenzweig in two different ways. He spoke of the religious man as possessing a "healthy understanding" and as having an appreciation for the significance of speech.

Rosenzweig conceived *The Star of Redemption* as an exegesis of what a living man would discover if he were truly open to the range and depth of human experience. The religious man who has been touched by revelation possesses this ability to be open, which Rosenzweig also designated as the healthy understanding. The man of common sense or healthy understanding knows that the road to understanding reality is not one of standing alone, abstracting isolated insights and combining these into a logical system. Man encounters the data of experience, God, the world, and other men in the process of living. His meetings or encounters with these elements teach him about the nature of reality in a way that is beyond being contested. The man of healthy understanding trusts his experiences, and these meetings give him a foundation for his life. A philosophy of plain, sound human understanding is thus the philosophy of man in all of his authenticity. In his essay "The New Thinking," Rosenzweig describes what it means to have this healthy posture toward the world and one's experiences. This is exemplified in the attitude which claims to know nothing more of the divine than what it has experienced—but to know this really, in the teeth of philosophy, which may brand this knowledge as "beyond" the "possible" experience; and nothing more of terrestrial matters than it has experienced . . . Such faith in experience might constitute the formulable element in the new thinking.[56]

In the small book *Understanding the Sick and the Healthy,* as we have seen, Rosenzweig identifies the sick understanding with the philosopher. What corrupts one's understanding is a mistrust of experience combined with the inability to wait for true meetings with God and with other men. The mistrust of experience leads to the disposition to rely totally on one's reason. Human reason, untouched by the outside world, is allowed to delineate the limits of experience and to determine the "hidden" facets of reality. Rather than living in the world and allowing the stream of experience to teach one of reality, the individual steps out of life and constructs a world. After his analysis of the sick understanding, exemplified by the philosopher, Rosenzweig prescribes the antidote to this malady: Health returns when one returns to the stream of life and events. Living fully in the world does not permit one to draw back and formulate systems of reality.[57]

Rosenzweig's analysis of the sick understanding and the necessary cure for this condition again brings to light his conception of the movement from philosophy to religion. Trust in the meaningfulness of life and in the truthfulness of his experiences is what the sick man lacked and what the healthy man possessed. This trust cannot come from man himself; but it is given through God's revelation to man. Trust is not difficult to maintain once one has experienced God's concern. With the knowledge that the Creator is also the one who cares for man, the individual can live fully within the stream of life.

Rosenzweig's philosophy of language provides another perspective into the relationship between philosophy and religion. The significance that he gives to language and to speech is based on his conviction that dialogue is both a human and a divine activity. As with love, the word is both of God and of man: "What man hears in his heart as his own human speech is the very word which comes out of God's mouth."[58] Rosenzweig's contention that the word is not just a human product has its basis in his understanding of the Bible. The Bible for Rosenzweig contains human words, but these words ultimately came from God. In addition, the Bible is not merely using anthropomorphisms when it describes the speech between man and God. Revelation is essentially dialogue according to Rosenzweig. It is a dialogue that is taken up day by day. In turning to man, God initiates this dialogue by expressing his love for man, calling man into relationship with Him, and commanding man to work in the world.

The divine/human character of speech discloses the continuity between the natural man and the religious man. Rosenzweig does not hold that before God's historic revelations man had no words. Language is "created from the beginning," but it "awakens to real vitality only in revelation."[59] Besides opening man up to the world, revelation brings man to trust in language. The lack of confidence in words was a major characteristic of philosophy in general and especially Idealism, according to Rosenzweig.[60] Philosophy, in taking reason as the highest faculty in man, believed that one had to be suspicious of language. Reality was not illumined by looking at language, for the rules of logic and mathematics were the governing rules of reality and world history. Language was seen as much too unsystematic. Thought had to go behind the words of the man on the street to get to the secret dialectic of reality.

In Rosenzweig's thought, language is the new organon. Rosenzweig holds that an analysis of grammar supplies the key to reality. Each particular form within language reflects one of the categories of reality. The order within language "appears as the original symbolism of reality itself and accordingly in the closest sense of 'identity' with this reality."[61] Language "describes the daily cosmic orbit of our planet along the zenith of world history,"[62] according to Rosenzweig. The sequences of reality, creation, revelation, and redemption are mirrored in grammar: creation—past tense, third person, indicative mood; revelation—present tense, second person, imperative mood;

redemption—future tense, first person, subjunctive mood.[63]

Creation is understood by man as an event in the past. One does not experience creation. Rather, one sees the finished products of this event. Creation is reflected in the world of things that is already there. One does not enter into dialogues of mutuality with the objects; one uses them. In creation even God speaks as an it. He is the source out of which things come. Thus, the past tense, the third person, and the indicative mood reflect the event of creation.

Revelation is mirrored in the present tense, the second person, and the imperative mood. Revelation is fully alive and present. The mutuality of dialogue and interaction of I and Thou brings both God and man into the living present. Rosenzweig wrote: "In the world of revelation everything becomes word, and what cannot become word is either prior to or posterior to this world."[64] Although Rosenzweig stresses the idea that in real dialogue both partners are changed, he sees that in the experiencing of God's word, man acts primarily as receiver. Revelation is experienced in God's command to love both Him and the neighbour. The imperative mood of language reminds one of God's command to love. Like all commands, the demand to love is only fully alive when it is addressed from a particular I to a listening and receptive Thou.

Redemption is something man neither has nor can yet experience. It is a promise about a world in the future. However, man knows of redemption because he can anticipate it. The life of men in community who together as a "we" address God, anticipates the redemption at the end of days. God's final act of redemption finds its symbol in the congregational prayer in which, speaking for all men, the group asks God to quickly bring in this new time.

For Rosenzweig, the movement from creation to revelation corresponds to the progress from man's life of monologue and the I-it world, to the life of dialogue, of I and Thou. This movement can also be described in terms of the passage from philosophy to religion. Philosophy reflects man's attempt to circumscribe everything within the I-it world of static thought. Rosenzweig held that philosophy is founded on the world of creation[65] where everything is treated as a finished object. Philosophy denies that mutual interaction and process are part of reality. The vision of the philosopher is tied to the past, where things can be manipulated and categorized by thought. On the other hand, the religious man lives in the present, where the basic nature of events as meetings is affirmed. In the present God and man are brought together by speech. Only speech makes God fully alive, that is, the Revealer, and man fully man, that is, one who accepts God's word and helps to establish it in the world. The individual who lives in the world of revelation thus knows the power of speech, according to Rosenzweig. Speech is the bridge between the elements, that which binds existence to existence.

## The Religious Person's Life in the World

The shift from the individual's initiation into the religious life to the life in the world, that is, from revelation to redemption, is marked in Rosenzweig's thought by the religious man's turning toward others. In the experience of revelation, man understands that God desires more than just a receiving soul. God also commands man to go back into the world and love his neighbour: "The love for God is to express itself in love for one's neighbor."[66] It is important to note that man is not just directed into the world, but into the human world. The response to God's call must at some time include the call to other men. The religious man is not permitted to close himself off from the other, as if he had never experienced God's love. He is asked to find the neighbour. In returning to the world, the other that one faces cannot remain an "it," like the rest of the world, something to be used and discarded. The neighbour is to be seen as a Thou, and in doing this the mutual transformation of I and Thou which was initiated by God is then repeated. Both persons discover that there is no authentic I unless it is able to communicate and to help a Thou. It is seen that the self is not fully alive unless it has become both a loving and beloved soul.

In turning toward the next one, the neighbour, the religious man is participating in the process of redemption. The transformation of the neighbour from "he" to a "thou" or soul also affects the world. As the religious man searches out the next one to allow his redemptive love to go out to him, love's power is also being planted in the world.[67] The exact nature of this ensouling of the world is not explored by Rosenzweig, who says that it is an "invisible" law.[68] At most, Rosenzweig suggests that man's love, by "a law operative in the order of the world by which things move toward man's act of love,"[69] sows the eternal into the world.

The religious person's active life in the world distinguishes him from the natural man who is frozen by the fear of death, and from the philosopher, who is under the stifling effect of philosophy. The ways of life of the natural man and the philosopher are both life-denying. Death denies the meaningfulness of life and one's work in the world. Once the individual is within its grasp, that is, the grasp of the fear of death, he cannot act in the world. This fear brings life to a halt, since the individual is hypnotized by the devastation that death will soon introduce. As we have seen, philosophy also takes man out of the stream of life. Thus, Rosenzweig called its *Weltanschauung* a premature death.[70] He spoke of two specific features of philosophy that engender this result. Philosophy tends to suggest that one cannot act in the world until the ultimate meaning of the universe is disclosed. Yet, according to Rosenzweig, the question of ultimate meaning is in fact only resolved in the process of living.[71] Philosophy also demeans human action by negating freedom, placing world history above human decision and action, and by replacing the *vita acta* with the *vita contemplativa*.

In defining revelation as orientation, as discussed earlier, Rosenzweig indicated how the religious life counters the thrusts of the fear of death and philosophy. Revelation gives the individual an overall understanding of the basic moments of reality, i.e. it points backward to creation and forward to redemption. Revelation allows man to act, for it enables the individual to trust in himself and the world, because the loving God of revelation upholds both.

Life in the world is a dialogue between God and man. In each particular situation the individual who is conscious of existing before God discovers he is being addressed by God. Escape from God's commands is impossible and thus man calls back. The individual now realizes that his life is filled with responsibility. God's commands, the personal and daily experience of the relevance of God's biblical commandments, give man authority over the world and over the ideals that are to be concretized in the world.[72]

The religious man's life in the world as an individual who lives with the neighbour and stands in dialogue with God discloses only two dimensions of the religious life. To understand the religious man one must also penetrate to his self-understanding and his experience as a member of a religious community. Actually, the previous discussion of the religious man in the world is somewhat misleading since it lacked this other feature. Rosenzweig speaks of the religious man only within the context of the Jewish and Christian communities. Only for Jews and Christians, according to Rosenzweig, has the fullness of God's revelation been appropriated into life. Other men have not yet been touched by God's ever-expanding love.

In the last section of *The Star of Redemption,* Rosenzweig brings together the personal experience of revelation with the individual's life within the religious community. The "I" of the religious man is grounded in more than its own experience. The religious man sees himself as a member of a community that continues to experience God as Revealer. Rosenzweig's vital interest in dialogue is not mitigated by this reference to the past. He suggests that the dialogue between the individual and God does not begin in a vacuum. The religious man's understanding of the present experience is shaped by God's past relations with the community. Thus, the community's traditions as well as the record of God's word in the Bible supplement and deepen the revelation to the single man.

The climax of the religious life, according to Rosenzweig, is the religious man's experience of eternity, an eternity which the community has brought into time. The core of this experience is the communal prayer. The community's plea for God's Kingdom allows the individual to feel eternity in the present and it also sows the seeds of the final redemption into the ever-growing-nearer future. Rosenzweig held that eternity is tied to the temporal as a result of the repetition of cultic holidays that enclose the sacred year. Within this year the moment is not allowed to pass away, but is caught and renewed again and again. For Rosenzweig this is the definition of eternity, that the moment becomes everlasting.[73]

Liturgy has a paradigmatic role in portraying redemption, as did speech or dialogue in Rosenzweig's understanding of revelation. Liturgy allows man to anticipate redemption by experiencing the "we" of the Kingdom in the present. It unites men through gestures in such a way that greater numbers are brought together and a deeper harmony is achieved than is possible through the dialogue of I and Thou. In addition, the power of the religious man's liturgical experiences strengthens him in accomplishing his work in the world.

Two fundamental dimensions of the relationship between philosophy and religion have been delineated up to this point. Rosenzweig characterizes this relationship as one of opposition, when philosophy and religion are treated as two conflicting ways of looking at man and the world. From the perspective of the life-history of the individual, Rosenzweig describes the movement from philosopher to religious man. At a central point in the *Star,* Rosenzweig introduces a third dimension of this relationship. He writes that to be a complete man living in the modern world, the individual must appropriate the insights of both the philosopher and the religious thinker or theologian. There is no ultimate validity to the battles between the philosopher and the theologian, because both express true aspects of man's living in the world. Only as both philosopher and theologian can the individual attain an insight into the Truth. The philosopher brings to the quest for truth the belief in the autonomy and integrity of the individual. He trusts only in what he can discover through his own powers and he insists that authenticity in existence depends upon remaining within his experiences of the purely human world. The theologian, the man who has encountered God, holds that a higher truth has been given to him. He can see beyond what his human eyes have revealed. Together as man of creation and man of revelation the individual becomes man in his highest state. Rosenzweig writes:

> God's truth conceals itself from those who reach for it with one hand only, regardless of whether the reaching hand is that of the objectivity of philosophers which preserves itself free of preconceptions, soaring above the objects, or that of the blindness of the theologians, proud of its experience and secluding itself from the world. God's truth wants to be entreated with both hands. It will not deny itself to him who calls upon it with the double prayer of the believer and the disbeliever. God gives of his wisdom to the one as to the other, to belief as well as to disbelief, but he gives to both only if their prayer comes before him united. It is the same man, disbelieving child of the world and believing child of God in one, who comes with dual plea and must stand with dual thanks before Him who gives of his wisdom to flesh and blood even as to those who fear him.[74]

Chapter III
# Martin Buber: The Movement Toward Dialogue

Martin Buber's portrait of the dialogue between God and man represents one of the great breakthroughs in modern religious thought. This breakthrough was the outcome of a long and sustained struggle. For two decades Buber sought to understand the nature of authentic living. During that time he embraced a number of different views concerning the relationship between the human and the divine. Only after an intense period of reflection upon past experiences and testing his conclusions against ever new encounters in the world did he forge the foundation of his revolutionary work, *I and Thou*. In *I and Thou* Buber spoke in a voice that hovered between poetry and prose about the "eternal Thou" that addresses man and directs him into the world.

As with Franz Rosenzweig, it is a problem reflecting "a state of perplexity, or even distress," rather than a question that is the driving force of Buber's early authorship. The great diversity of these early writings—including studies of mysticism, myth, legends, Zionism, Hasidism, as well as his own philosophical reflections—cannot disguise the fact that a single burning problem energized him. The quest to uncover the deepest springs of authentic human living led Buber to explore the nature of human life as well as the relationships between man, nature, and God. With the publication of *I and Thou* in 1923, Buber offered the hard won insight that the total expanse of the human is only brought to fulfillment by those who engage in dialogue with other men, with nature, with the world of art, and with God.

Several critics, as well as Buber himself, have depicted the early religious reflections in terms of three stages.[1] During a period of time that roughly coincides with the first decade of the twentieth century Buber spoke of a mystical unification of man and God, that is, of the "unification of the self with the all-self."[2] This idea was then rejected in favor of the truth of "realization" (*Verwirklichung*). Buber held that one must "live so as to realize God in all things."[3] Finally, between the years 1919 and 1922 he reached a standpoint which he was never to abandon. Buber understood that "the relation to a human being is the proper metaphor for the relation to God—as genuine address is here accorded a genuine answer."[4]

The following pages will trace the relationship between man and God in Buber's thought from his earliest works through the writing of *I and Thou*. This evolving thought process mirrors Buber's own struggles to uncover the full meaning of man's life in the world. The first fragmentary solutions ripened over time in conjunction with the author's own maturation. At the end of this process Buber was able to both find himself and to guide others. Buber has offered the following overview of this movement:

> Since I have matured to a life from my own experience—a process that began shortly before the "First World War" . . . I have stood under the duty to insert the framework of the decisive experiences that I had at that time into the human inheritance of thought . . .[5]

Buber's exploration of some of the most important dimensions of man's religious experience brought forward something new as well as partaking of the old. The transformation or conversion within Buber's thinking about God was also a reintegration of his earlier reflections. In an effort to guide his readers through the maze of some of the early writings, Buber wrote in 1923 that he had gone through a process of "clarification" in which "my words became clear to myself."[6] The "clarification" should be taken in the double sense that not only are the seeds of the theme of *I and Thou* within the earlier writings, but that there are vital continuities between the earlier and later standpoints. Again, as with Rosenzweig, the movement from the earlier to the later stance meant a reintegration or "clarification" rather than a repudiation of the past. However, at the end of this chapter we will see that those fragments from Buber's past positions threaten the purity of the voice of dialogue that resounds in *I and Thou*.

## I. Mysticism and the Philosophy of Realization

Martin Buber was born in Vienna in 1878. At the age of three his parents separated and he went to live with his grandparents in Galicia. Buber's later reminiscences of this period with his grandparents are very positive. In some autobiographical fragments Buber writes that he learned what "love for the genuine word" was from his scholarly grandfather and from his sensitive grandmother.[7] Buber often spent the summers with his father and was greatly impressed by his relationship with nature. During these years Buber also encountered the power and wholeness of Eastern European Jews, especially the Hasidim who brought a mystic fervor into all of their life. He left this setting in his fourteenth year, in order to pursue formal studies. At the same time he ceased observing Jewish law. In 1896, at the age of eighteen, Martin enrolled at the University of Vienna. He studied some summers at the University of Berlin, where his teachers included Wilhelm Dilthey and Georg Simmel.

Martin Buber's early writings, from the period he was completing his university degree through the second decade of this century, reflect a pervasive sense of alienation and a concomitant desire for unity and harmony. Buber was haunted by a feeling of being alienated from the world and from his true self. The expressions of this alienation are unmistakable, but their source or sources are not fully evident. Buber's passionate quest for unity seems to have come about from the merging of personal event and temperament with the general intellectual climate of the time. In a recent reflection on his earliest years, Buber spoke of the growing effect that his separation from his mother had on him. While still a young man he began to universalize this experience, stating "I had begun to perceive it as something that concerned not only me, but all men."[8] Some critics have also pointed to the early death of a childhood friend as having a strong effect on this sensitive young person.[9] In addition, he shared the overpowering sense of alienation expressed by many young people at that time. An influential segment of youth throughout Europe felt estranged from the world of their time. They believed that a "true" community life was impossible in the modern world and that bourgeois culture and values were in great part responsible for this. The immense devastation of World War I heightened the feeling of *angst*.[10]

Jewish youth, in particular, felt alienated from their surroundings. In many cases they were cut off from the social and cultural life of the nations in which they resided. Yet a return to the traditional Jewish community of the *shtetl* was neither desired nor possible. There was a deep rift between the generations of European Jewry at this time. The sons often looked with horror at the materialistic and rationalistic lives of their fathers. Many young Jews passionately rejected their parents' ways and sought new paths toward authenticity.[11]

Buber found some consolation, as did many of his generation in the intellectual resurgence of romanticism. Three dimensions of the neo-romantic climate had a very strong appeal for him. First, he was attracted by the great interest in mysticism. The highest mystic experience that uncovered the unity of the individual with God and the world, seemed to answer the need for harmony within and without. Second, Buber had a great appreciation for the powers of the creative life of the artist. Here Nietzsche's portrait of the bold creative individual was of immense influence. Nietzsche extolled the inner powers of the individual who could venture beyond the dead and fragmented present to bring forth a new world and a new self. Third, the quest for a "true" community led Buber and others to glorify the folk communities of the premodern period. The organic tie between community and land as well as the myths that brought men and nature together were immensely attractive for many of this generation.

The first of Buber's three intellectual stages has been designated by him and by many of his critics as the mystical phase. His writings during the first decade of the twentieth century have a homogeneity brought about by an all-consuming quest for "unification." Many years later Buber introduced a small piece that he had written in 1910 with a comment that accurately depicts his first understanding of the manner in which man can overcome the disharmony both within the self and between the self and the world.

> One may call it the "mystical" phase if one understands as mystic the belief in a unification of the self with the all-self, attainable by man in levels or intervals of his earthly life. Underlying this belief, when it appears in its true form, is usually a genuine "ecstatic" experience.[12]

Aspects of both religious and aesthetic experience were the source of Buber's pantheism at this time. There was a blending of the insight of the nature mystic with the experience of aesthetic creativity of the poet. Life in the everyday world was deprecated in favor of the extraordinary ecstatic vision. The religious was for him the "exception," that which allowed one to escape the everyday. In reflecting back on this period Buber has written that "the 'religious' lifted you out. Over there now lay the accustomed existence with its affairs, but here illumination and ecstasy and rapture held without time or sequence."[13]

The fragmented self and the estrangement of the individual from the universe were the points of departure for this standpoint. Particular experiences, however, brought one to understand that the fragmentation and alienation were not ultimate. If the individual seeker experienced any one thing in all of its fullness, then the unity of all that exists became apparent. While God was found within all things, he was best understood as that pervasive unity of the whole. Like man, the things of the universe longed for God, that is, they longed to overcome divisiveness and to become integrated into God.

## 50  What Does Revelation Mean for the Modern Jew?

There is a major difficulty that stands in the way of every effort to examine the writings of Buber's authorship, and this is particularly true in regard to the works of his first, "mystical," phase. Words that present Buber's ideas in his own name are relatively few, compared to the great number of interpretations of other thinkers and investigations of various religious traditions and movements. However, these diverse interpretative writings do offer a rich field for uncovering Buber's own thoughts.[14] Buber treats only topics that are very close to him, that is, that offer some kind of resolution to the problems that drive him. In addition, for Buber interpretations and investigations are relished as opportunities to recreate what lies before him from out of the depths of his own inner truths. Although this tendency to recreate is somewhat mitigated in later years, a statement of 1907 in relation to his treatment of Hasidic legends reveals Buber's creative interest in and use of material. He writes, "I bear in me the blood and spirit of those who created it, and out of my blood and spirit it has become new."[15]

Buber's first works explored the relationship between the multiplicity of created things and the unity of God. Mystics, especially the major German mystics Meister Eckhart and Jacob Boehme, provided the answers to this relationship between the One and the Many. Buber's doctoral dissertation at the University of Vienna in 1904 dealt with the problem of individuation in the thought of mystics from Nicholas of Cusa to Jacob Boehme. In his treatment of the figures of Cusa and Boehme, he ignored the Christian elements and highlighted their pantheistic tendencies. For example, with Cusa, Buber focused on the idea that all beings participate in God and that the more they develop, the greater is that participation. He felt close to Boehme's conception of creation as an on-going process in which God participates and eventually brings all things into unity with Himself.[16]

Other writings of this period indicate Buber's fascination with the idea that God *becomes* through the processes of the universe. In his first important essay "Ueber Jakob Boehme" of 1901, Buber indicates his own interest in the problem of the relationship between the individual and the world, and he resolves this question by again speaking of the "becoming God." He sees that there is an inner longing of all things for unity and that through this longing "all beings are united to God . . . and it is the way to the new God whom we create, to the new unity of forces."[17]

This remains Buber's point of view until 1910. Man's power to bring about the unity of things in God is reiterated in his presentation of ecstatic religious experiences in 1909, *Ekstatische Konfessionen*.[18] One of Buber's later reflections summarizes the point of view that reigned at this time in his thought. He wrote:

> Since 1900 I had first been under the influence of German mysticism from Meister Eckhart to Angelus Silesius, according to which the primal ground (*Ungrund*) of being, the nameless impersonal godhead, comes to "birth" in the human soul.[19]

At the same time that Buber was writing about German mysticism, he was being slowly drawn from an individualistic solution to the problem of alienation toward a more community-oriented treatment. The interest in community was not completely foreign to Buber's earliest writings, since the quest for a true community was central to that resurgence of romanticism that had so much influence on him. However, a number of factors contributed to the deepening of this focus on the community. First, Buber's commitment to socialism grew over the years, especially following World War I. Second, in 1897 Buber became an active member of the newly emergent Zionist movement. Zionism deepened his interest in man's life within community and led him to explore the nature, as well as the future, of Judaism.[20] Third, Buber's reacquaintance with Hasidism in 1904 taught him of the redemptive quality of communal life. His writings on this mass mystical movement always take the sacral quality of the relationship between the leader, or *Zaddik,* and his followers, the Hasidim, as a primary focal point.

It would be wrong to leave the impression that Buber was guided in a totally new direction. The philosophy of dialogue lies far in the future at this point in his life. However, Buber's renewed contact with Hasidism did have an immediate effect, according to him. In language strongly parallel to the descriptions of religious conversion, Buber once said that "It was then that, overpowered in an instant, I experienced the Hasidic soul. The primally Jewish opened to me . . ."[21]

Two works on Hasidism, *Die Geschichte des Rabbi Nacham* of 1906 and *Die Legend des Baalschem* of 1908, reveal Buber's continual emphasis on ecstatic experience as the liberating path out of alienation and separation. In the latter book there is an extensive treatment of the category of *hitlahavut*, that is, ecstasy. For Buber ecstasy is the *via regna* that leads to the All or God. Ecstatic experience allows one to soar beyond all limits, beyond the worldly and divided, beyond time, nature and thought. Through it one comes "to the I of God, the simple unity and boundlessness"[22] and stands there. *Hitlahavut* is nothing less than "the envelopment in God beyond time and space."[23] Buber also speaks of the great man who lives in the world with others and helps them to establish fulfilling community. However, it is still ecstasy, in which one rises above all activity in the world, that is proclaimed as the highest value. In fact, even the passion of ecstasy is left behind in the final immersion in God; "only he who sinks into the Nothing of the Absolute receives the forming hand of spirit."[24]

The term "realization" (*Verwirklichung*) best characterizes the second stage of Buber's thought. This term is omnipresent in Buber's work from 1910 to 1914, and its primacy is clearly evidenced by the title of his first full philosophical statement, *Daniel: Dialogues on Realization*. While the transition from his "mystical" period to his thought on "realization" is distinct, the factors that lie behind this development are, once again, open to diverse judgments.

Buber, as much as any religious thinker since Soren Kierkegaard, indicates that ground that he has traversed by discussing the errors of those positions that he had earlier held. In the many places that he reexamines the view that ecstatic experience leads to the unification with God, Buber offers the critique that such ecstatic experience degrade's man's life in the world. His belief that life should not be split up between the inauthenticity of being in the world and the liberation of ecstasy, seems to have led him to seek the end of human alienation in a way of life rather than in some supreme moments of passion.

While the goal of unity between man and God remains, Buber's view of the road to this unity undergoes alteration. God is now seen to be brought to fulfillment through the active life, through man's deeds. Ecstatic contemplation is held to be too static to truly bring together the I and the Other. At a later time, Buber saw this change in the following way. After being influenced by German mysticism to the extent that he believed that "the nameless, impersonal godhead, comes to 'birth' in the human soul," he then

> had been under the influence of the later Kabbala and of Hasidism, according to which man has the power to unite the God who is over the world with his *shekinah* dwelling in the world. In this way there arose in me the thought of a realization of God through man; man appeared to me as the being through whose existence the Absolute, resting in its truth, can gain the character of reality.[25]

Buber frequently refers to God during this period as "the Unconditioned" (*Unbedingten*), or as the Absolute. God was conceived as something that dwelled in the world as a world spirit. God, as a dimension of the world, could be heightened or "realized" through man's embracing and finding the latent unity of all things.

The philosophy of "realization" begins to take shape in Buber's earliest addresses on Judaism and in his epilogue to the translation of the sayings of Chuang-tzu, "The Teaching of Tao." The first three speeches or addresses on Judaism were delivered from 1909 to 1911 to a Zionist youth group in Prague, the Bar Kokhba Circle.[26] There is a uniform portrayal of Judaism and its relationship to the human condition in all of the speeches. Buber affirms that the alienation that the Jew has experienced and continues to experience is the most poignant example of mankind's universal condition. In its essence Judaism reflects man's twofold fragmentariness. The individual is not whole and he is also cut off from the world. As a consequence of the Jew's intense alienation, Judaism also represents the deepest struggle of man to overcome his "primal dualism." The transformation of man and the world is accomplished through the "striving for unity." In fact, what men know as God or the divine is a product of this struggle for harmony and wholeness. Buber writes, for example:

> [the Jew] had drawn Him not out of reality but out of his own yearning, because he had not espied Him in heaven or earth but had established Him as a unity above his own duality, as salvation above his own suffering.[27]
>
> It is this striving for unity that has made the Jew creative. Striving to evolve unity out of the division of his I, he conceived the idea of the unitary God.[28]

The familiar refrain of the quest for unity reverberates throughout the short introductory piece of 1910, "The Teaching of Tao."[29] Buber affirms here that unity is not the result of either thought or emotion. Unity is the achievement of the individual who is able to create or elicit unity out of the multiplicity of things. The great master takes up all things of the world into his life and brings all together into an unconditioned whole.[30] Buber writes that it is the perfected man's "unity that sets unity in the world."[31] The great masters saw that "nothing other than human life . . . is the bearer of all transcendence."[32]

In describing the Way or Tao of life that is all-inclusive, Buber suggests that it also transcends action and speech. No particular action or group of actions leads to unity. The Way of the perfected man will necessarily appear as nonaction (*Nichttun*), when observed by the ordinary man. Speech too, which introduces the divisive, is opposed to the silence of the "unified man." In bringing together the themes of the inner harmony of the perfected man and the necessity of silence, Buber holds that in the wordless depths of the unified man there is "no Thou other than the I."[33]

The book *Daniel: Dialogues on Realization,*[34] published in 1913, is Buber's finest and most powerful statement of the philosophy of realization. This book is an important signpost on the road to Buber's later philosophy of dialogue. *Daniel* is the first book that explores his own philosophical views rather than just weaving his views into the interpretations of other thinkers and the presentation of religious movements and texts. The style and structure of *Daniel* is startling. The auther does not seek to argue or even to delineate his position as much as to offer and rhapsodize about the meaning of his experiences. Within the five "dialogues" that make up this work, the familiar topic of the relationship between duality and unity is of primary significance.

Daniel, the main character or speaker of the book, affirms that duality is the basic fact of life. The child and youth may not be aware of the omnipresent duality, but the mature person cannot escape it. There is an "abyss" between all things in the universe: "spirit and matter, form and material, being and becoming, reason and will, positive and negative element."[35] At one place Daniel concludes that "he who genuinely experiences the world experiences it as a duality."[36] However, this conclusion only points forward to man's real "task," which is the overcoming of the tension between the I and the multiplicity of things.

The meaning of realization, as well as the distance Buber has come from his previous understandings of the religious life, is illuminated by the manner in which the "task" of unity is fulfilled. The key fifth dialogue, "On Unity: Dialogue by the Sea," begins with a description of the "three wrong ways" that unity is sought. First, there is that "wisdom which commanded one to strip off the world of duality as the world of appearance."[37] Here Buber repudiates that way of achieving unity that demands that the self strip off all apparent dualities until it sees itself as included in the unity of All.[38] This method, of the Vedanta nondualist school of Hinduism, is rejected because it annihilates one's everyday experiences of living in the world. Second, there is that "wisdom that thought duality together into unity."[39] This position, which has been identified by critics as German Idealism, holds that despite the seeming conflict of things in the universe, the wise man knows that all are ultimately one, that is, that there is an identity of each with the All. This answer too is denied by Buber, because this identity is not confirmed by man's day to day life in the world. Additionally, the individual is not comforted by such an esoteric knowing. Third, there is the way of "the awakened man who indifferentiates all opposites and all antinomies in himself."[40] Here one is reminded of Buber's earlier treatment of Taoism. This position is also rejected, because it leads to a deadening of life rather than to an intensification of living in the world. The conclusion that follows from the denial of the three ways is that unity must be achieved so that the uniqueness, as well as the heights and depths of experiencing are included. The individual must "live through the tension [of duality] in the world," and from out of that tension create unity.[41]

There are hints in the above solution that *Daniel* is only a waystation and not the final destination of Buber's religious quest. Without reading backward from *I and Thou,* it is still clear that the relationship between the "I" and individual things in the world has not been fully worked out. On the one hand, Buber believes that it is an error to identify the "I" of the individual with the totality of the universe. The soul is realized only by *living* the tension between things and not by merging with the world. On the other hand, unity remains the goal, since ultimately the individual realizes the unity of All within the self. Buber writes that "everything individual is only preparation."[42] The dialectic of these two sides of the struggle for unity is laid bare in the following lines:

> True unity cannot be found, it can only be created. He who creates it realizes the unity of the world in the unity of his soul. Thus beforehand he must live through the tension of the world in his soul as his own soul's tension.[43]

There is a strong romantic thrust to *Daniel,* despite its rejection of ecstasy and German Idealism. The creative power of the "I" is extolled as the architect of the highest reality. While the "I" may no longer be identical with the "All," as with Hegel, it still brings forth the elemental unity of the whole. Continuing in this vein, Buber holds that the soul's creative response to the hidden dimension of every thing results in God's realization. Thus, "he who has direction and meaning celebrates an ever-new mystery in his realizing: to live so as to realize God in all things."[44]

The theme of God's realization through man's unconditioned activity is reaffirmed in the second series of Buber's "Addresses" on Judaism. These, once again, reveal Buber's strong tie to the neo-romantic current of his time. He opposes the qualities of the "Orient" to those of the "Occident;" religious feeling to stagnant religious forms; and he frequently explores the role of myth in the life of the organic community or *Volk*. In harmony with the underlying outlook of these views, the creative individual's powers are extended until they include the potentiality of realizing God.

In "The Spirit of the Orient and Judaism,"[45] of 1912, the Jew is offered as the representative Oriental man who feels the duality of existence and who confronts this duality through action. He acts to transform alienation into unity. "Jewish Religiosity," of 1913, affirms that the doctrine of God's realization through man is taught by Judaism.[46] Biblical texts are utilized by Buber to demonstrate that this understanding of the relationship between God and man is to be found in the Bible itself, although he argues that the "unique character of Jewish religiosity" has been covered over by "rabbinism and rationalism."[47] For example, the *Genesis* statement that man is created in the image of God is interpreted to mean that "God is man's goal," and that God's realization is accomplished by imitating His unity and unconditionality.[48] Isaiah's famous declaration that the Jews are God's witnesses (Isa. 43:10) is said to refer to "God's realization through an intensification of His reality."[49] Put in another way, through the unconditioned deed, that is, the deed that arises out of the highest "power of decision" and "sanctity of intent,"[50] man experiences his "communion with God."[51]

In these addresses there is frequent reference to Hasidism. The portrait of Hasidism of this period mirrors Buber's understanding of the nature of true religious life in general. Whereas at an earlier time religious ecstasy, *hitlahavut,* was proclaimed as

Hasidism's highest value, it is now the life of decision and realization that is said to be the essence of this religious movement. In "Myth in Judaism," delivered in 1914, Buber writes that Hasidism emphasized the power of the man who "lives from his very core."[52] It teaches that the divine is revealed in the world by the deeds of those men who turn to the world and act to liberate the hidden dimension of all things.[53]

In reflecting back upon his early intellectual development, Buber recognized 1914 as a turning point. He wrote that it was in that year that he recognized that the dialogue between the individual and the other was not a monologue of the self with itself. However, this fundamental insight of his later philosophy of dialogue took another five years (1919) "to ripen to expression."[54]

The small essay "With a Monist"[55] perhaps best represents Buber's stance of 1914 and the ground that still had to be traversed. "With a Monist," like *Daniel,* takes the form of a dialogue. However, unlike the latter, it reflects the liveliness of a true dialogue of give and take. The discussion is between an unnamed protagonist and a "monist." The protagonist begins by denying that he is a mystic, that is, one who negates the actuality of things in the world and who denies reason's claim to fathom any dimension of the world. The protagonist holds that reality must be heightened and not annihilated and that reason has a legitimate claim to grasp aspects, but not the totality, of the universe. In some ways the essay proposes views that have been offered by Buber in earlier pieces. There is the familiar call to experience the world intensely and thereby to bring to light a new dimension of reality:

> Reality is no fixed condition, but a quantity which can be heightened . . . And how can I give this reality to my world except by seeing the seen with all the strength of my life, hearing the heard with all the strength of my life . . .[56]

Also present is the task to create unity: "any true deed brings, out of lived unity, unity into the world."[57]

Yet there is a powerful *new* note that sounds throughout this short piece: a deep concern for the integrity of the particular thing, which is said to address the sensitive human subject. The object that one turns to is described as "the unique," and "at the moment of experience nothing else exists."[58] In addition, the things of the world are no longer seen as totally passive elements to be reworked into a higher synthesis. The object is permitted an active dimension: "their activity, their effective reality, reveals itself" to the subject.[59]

This regard for the integrity of the particular thing completely overshadows whatever hints in earlier writings there were to that effect. In *Daniel* the particularity of each thing was acknowledged, but this uniqueness was not allowed to stand since "nothing individual is real in itself: everything individual is only preparation."[60] While the task of realizing the unity of the particulars remains viable in "With a Monist," there is now a heightened tension between this task and the unique voice of every thing. We find, for example, that

> He who truly experiences a thing so that it springs up to meet him and embraces him of itself has in that thing known the world.[61]

> In the features of the beloved [the things to which the loving man turns], whose self he realizes, he discerns the enigmatic countenance of the universe.[62]

The word "God" does not appear in this very significant essay. However, it is not unreasonable to suspect that as Buber recognized the uniqueness and integrity of the things of the universe, he saw that God could not merely remain a dimension of these things. Buber never refers to any particular religious experience during these years that brought him to recognize the true otherness of God. The student of Buber's thought is left to carefully probe into the early writings to uncover lines of development as well as turning points in Buber's treatment of man's relationship to God. Buber's new understanding of the world and its otherness, as reflected in "With a Monist," does give evidence that a different view of man's relationship to God is in the offing.

## 60  What Does Revelation Mean for the Modern Jew?

As was stated earlier, Buber saw the period around World War I as a turning point in his thought. In addition to the impact of the tremendous destruction of human life that occurred during the war, there were two particular discussions in which Buber took part that helped to bring about his movement toward the philosophy of dialogue. The first of these is discussed in Buber's essay of 1929, "Dialogue," under the heading of "A Conversion."[63] Buber recounts that "one forenoon, after a morning of 'religious' enthusiasm, I had a visit from an unknown young man, without being there in spirit." Buber was friendly and attentive, but he severely criticized himself later, after he found out from a friend of the young man's that this person was killed in the war. Buber recognized that he had not tried to fathom what really was behind the young person's spoken inquiries and that, most of all, he had not stood face to face with him as someone concerned, someone truly present. From that time on, Buber affirmed, he repudiated his earlier philosophical view that ignored the concrete everyday world of people.

The second encounter was with an old friend and extremely important young socialist thinker, Gustav Landauer, concerning Buber's first, enthusiastic reactions to the outbreak of the war. In a number of letters and a later series of conversations that took place in July 1916, Landauer strongly criticized Buber's attempts to see the death and destruction of the war as opportunities for young men to be freed from the routine and everyday and to live a life of ultimate risk for the sake of the "unconditioned." Landauer sarcastically spoke of Buber as the "Kriegsbuber," and insisted that he acknowledge the illusions of his mixture of German nationalism and the mysticism of experience (*Erlebnis*).[64]

The critic who discovered this correspondence between Buber and Landauer, Paul Flohr, regarded this encounter between the two friends as a decisive turning point in Buber's way to his later philosophy. Flohr recognized "three new elements" in Buber's thought after the spring of 1916, which he believed were strongly influenced by this event:

a) an explicit opposition to the war and chauvinistic nationalism; b) a reevaluation of the function and meaning of *Erlebnis;* c) a shift in the axis of *Gemeinschaft* (community) from consciousness . . . to the relations between men.[65]

In the following pages we will explore those writings that provide the immediate background for *I and Thou*. According to Buber, the first draft of this seminal work was written in 1919 and the final work was completed in 1922.[66] Buber's works of 1918 and 1919 reveal the last movements in Buber's development, since they are close in time as well as in thought to his philosophy of dialogue.

During the years that immediately precede *I and Thou* Buber devoted much of his time to reading and writing on Hasidism. Buber clearly believed that his work on Hasidic material was one of the most important sources of his developing philosophy of dialogue.[67] In the autobiographical fragment, "My Way to Hasidism" (1918), Buber summarizes the teachings of this movement in the sentence, "God can be beheld in each thing and reached through each pure deed."[68] This statement is followed by the important clarification that "this insight is by no means to be equated with a pantheistic world view . . ."[69] There is still a great distance between his thinking in this essay and *I and Thou*. God is not referred to here as a separate "Thou" who confronts man. Thus, for example, the pure deed is said to be "wholly directed to God and concentrated in Him."[70]

Many minor chords that resound in two more addresses on Judaism in the years 1918 and 1919 evidence the metamorphasis in Buber's thought. The first address, "The Holy Way,"[71] is given in memory of Gustav Landauer. Buber's increasing preoccupation with Hasidism and the friendship with Landauer deepened his early interest in the redeeming features of true community. "The Holy Way," consequently, emphasizes the importance of the life of man with man. The focus on the relationship between people might be responsible for a subtle shift in the conception of the divine-human relationship. Buber writes that "true human life is conceived to be a life lived in the presence of God."[72] More metaphorically, we find that God "speaks out of the present, out of the *Urim* and *Tummim* of our innermost hearts."[73] This life in the presence of God or in response to the voice of God is not as clear a departure from Buber's early thought as it may first appear. God is a dimension of human reality that can be realized through authentic life with other men. God is "an elementary present spiritual reality . . . emanating from the immediacy of existence as such."[74] While Buber distinguishes himself from those who seek to find God "within all things" of the world, he affirms that God "must be realized between them."[75] He writes:

> The Divine may come to life in individual man, may reveal itself from within individual man; but it attains its earthly fullness only where, having awakened to an awareness of their universal being, individual beings open themselves to one another . . .[76]

"The Holy Way" thus presents a clear view of Buber's developing understanding of man's relationship to God. God is not a hypothesis of thought nor is He fully accessible to the mystic who seeks to ferret him out by seeing Him in the things of the world. The repudiation here of a nature mysticism and of a view that God is to be found through some intense, ecstatic experiences is significant. Yet, as stated before, God is never directly addressed as a "Thou." He "emanates" or is "realized" through the relationship between man and man. Buber himself is not content to stand by a statement that describes God's place in the world in the following way: "God is content to reside in the realm between one earthly being and the other."[77]

Finally, "The Holy Way" reflects a few stylistic and thematic currents that point to changes in Buber's thought at this time. His use of Biblical passages is both more pronounced and more circumspect in these later years. He no longer uses such passages as proof texts for his ideas by taking them out of their historical and experiential contexts. Where there is an allusion to mysticism, the reference takes on a negative tone.[78] Additionally, the word "the Unconditioned" is not as pervasive as before. The word "God" has begun to replace this earlier favorite.

Buber once reflected that he came to "decisive clarity" just after completing the address of 1919, "Herut: On Youth and Religion."[79] Within "Herut" the tension between the two competing stances that we have been tracing is almost at a bursting point. God is both a "Thou" who addresses men and He is the highest dimension of the interhuman life. These two positions are reconciled by the problematic phrase, "freedom in God" (*Freiheit in Gott*).[80]

Buber has never spoken of God's presence before man with as much intensity. Even though utilizing the term "the unconditional" Buber writes: "Man's mind thus experiences the unconditional as that something that is counterposed against it, as the Thou as such."[81] God calls man and it is of primary importance that man live so that he can "confront his Caller."[82] In particular, Buber tells his audience that they must be part of the ongoing generations of the Jewish community by responding fully to God's call. He speaks of community as the repository of "mankind's wordless dialogue with God."[83]

Despite the foregoing and an attack by Buber upon those who find God by savouring some great personal experience (*Erlebnis*), God still seems to be reduced to a dimension of human reality. Although the unconditioned is a "Thou as such," the mind experiences the unconditional within itself.[84] Even the "wordless dialogue" that takes place between the community and God can be found "condensed . . . into the language of the soul."[85]

The phrase "freedom in God" allows Buber to speak of God as other than man, while also permitting him to return to the view that God is not fully distinct from man. Thus, one finds that religion's "true task" is

> man's response to the Divine, the response of the total human being; hence, the unity of the spiritual and the worldly, the realization of the spirit, and the spiritualization of the worldly;

the sanctification of the relationship to all things, that is, freedom in God.[86]

At the same time that Buber was working on the first draft of *I and Thou* he gave his attention to another work on Hasidism, *The Great Maggid and His Followers.* The "Introduction" (1919) to this work is the climax of his maturing thought about Hasidism. The "Introduction" is animated by the ripening understanding of the divine-human encounter.[87]

The departure from earlier presentations of Hasidism is multifaceted. In the writings on Hasidism of the first decade, especially *The Legend of the Baal Shem* (1908), ecstasy or *hitlahavut,* was revered as the highest of values. Ecstasy is now reduced to a mere gateway of the true Hasidic life.[88] Even more strongly, Buber describes the ascetic ecstasy as coming from the demonic, rather than from the divine, side of man.[89] This new statement of Hasidic teaching also stands in contrast to that understanding of Hasidism that accentuated the realization of the divine in the world through human activity.[90] As we will soon see, the word "meeting" replaces the earlier key term "realization."

The treatment of the concept of unification is also a departure from the past. Unification no longer refers to man's uniting with the All or with God. Buber limits the use of this term to either the becoming one of God with Himself, that is, the unification of God and the *Shekinah,* or the unification of man's inner life. Corresponding to the latter we find that the Hasidic leader or *Zaddik* is the one "whose forces, purified and united" seeks salvation for all men and all ages.[91]

Finally, there is a significant effort by Buber to dissociate Hasidism from its precursor, *Kabbalah,* especially from its magical side.[92] In the past the continuities between these two Jewish mystical expressions were accentuated. Buber's new view about the Hasidic teaching of the meeting between God and man leads him to sharply delineate the boundaries between Hasidism and the earlier, more clearly immanental, mystical tradition.[93]

Buber forcefully affirms that the event of *meeting* between God and man is the goal of Hasidic life, as well as the *telos* of all authentic religious life. Hasidism purified some of the elements of the *Kabbalah* and thus gave a new intensity to the teaching that man's responsibility for the universe has its foundation in the meeting between God and man.[94] This characterization of the nature and course of man's activity in the world is also attributed by Buber to Judaism and all religious movements. He writes that the Jewish teaching is "wholly based upon the double-directional relation of the human I and the divine Thou, on the reality of reciprocity, on the *meeting*."[95] In fact, "all genuine religious movements" agree with this view, for they seek to show man "the path on which he can meet God."[96]

From the time that *Daniel* was writtin in 1912 we have seen the increasing role that man's work in the world plays in Buber's philosophy of religion and in his portraits of various religious movements. In the "Introduction" to *The Great Maggid and His Followers* this dimension of his thought is even more pronounced. Hasidism does not focus on magical or sacral activity, but on "the hallowing of the everyday."[97] As against those who acclaim the present experience of the divine as the *summum bonum* of religious life, Hasidism presents a much more dynamic understanding of the nature of redemption. It stresses action and responsibility for the future, and in this way it renews life and turns toward the Creator.[98] No earlier formulation of Hasidic teaching rivals the dynamic that Buber now wishes to give to its views about acting in the world.

Despite these changes, in Buber's analysis of the concept of *yihud*, unification, there remains a tension between his developing thought about meeting and his prior positions. As was discussed beforehand, Buber speaks of the unification of God with Himself and of the unification of man's inner life. The fact that the divine is not just an aspect of the human is, of course, a presupposition of any understanding of the divine-human *meeting*. Buber makes this point repeatedly in *I and Thou*. Yet, in the present work there are places where the distinction between the divine and the human begins to melt away. In some long passages one finds that

## 66 What Does Revelation Mean for the Modern Jew?

> *Yihud* means . . . the divine element living in man moves from him to God's service, to God's intention, to God's work; God, in whose name and by whose command of creation the free *yihud* takes place, is his goal and end, he himself turning not in himself but to God, not isolated, but swallowed in the world process, no circle but the swinging back of the divine strength that was sent forth.[99]

> Here, in genuine prayer, there appears most clearly the essential meaning of *yihud,* that it is no "subjective" happening, but the dynamic form of the divine unity itself. "The people imagine," says Rabbi Pinhas of Koretz, "that they pray before God. But this is not so. For prayer itself is the essence of divinity."[100]

In these passages the separation between God and man is blurred and the actuality of the meeting between God and man is in danger of losing its impact. The ambiguities arise when Buber looks at man in the wider context of the cosmos and when he describes the highest secret of prayer. In these examples the dialogue between God and man dissipates into a divine monologue of God with Himself. At a later place in this chapter we will reexamine this danger and determine whether it is finally overcome in the philosophy of *I and Thou.*

The publication of some pivotal lectures given by Buber in 1922 allows us to examine the period immediately preceding the publication of *I and Thou.*[101] From January 15 to March 12, 1922, Buber undertook a series of eight lectures on "Religion as Presence" at the *Freies Jüdisches Lehrhaus* in Frankfort that was headed by Franz Rosenzweig. These lectures indicate that Buber was closer to his writings on "realization" and further from the philosophy of dialogue in *I and Thou* than one might suppose. Buber still uses the term "realization" extensively. He affirms, for example, that the "Thou" which confronts the individual must be "realized" rather than just "experienced."[102] He still speaks of man realizing God in the world.[103] In addition, the idea of dialogue is present only in the most minimal way.

Rivka Horwitz, the critic responsible for publishing these extremely important essays, also describes Buber's discussions and exchange of letters with Franz Rosenzweig in the months prior to the completed draft of *I and Thou*.[104] Horwitz especially sees Rosenzweig's influence on Buber in terms of the replacement of realization with a deep understanding of dialogue. After describing the correspondence between these two thinkers which starts in September 1922, she concludes:

> This entire correspondence leaves no doubt that Buber's book on dialogue was written in the midst of a most significant living dialogue on its themes. Rosenzweig's influence can no longer be doubted; only its extent may be differently evaluated.[105]

One of the most important sources for our study of Buber's developing thought has been his addresses, *Reden,* on Judaism. We have carefully traced the transformations in the understanding of the relationship between God and man from the first address of 1909 to "Herut" of 1919. As Buber declared, it was shortly after this last address that he gained full clarity of vision, in the process of writing and reworking *I and Thou.* Buber's "Preface" of 1923 to the eight addresses on Judaism provides a fitting conclusion to the first section of this chapter.[106]

The "Preface" acts as a warning to his readers, a warning that prevents the uninitiated from plunging directly into the addresses. Buber was compelled to indicate his present understanding (1923), before having his readers go on to his earlier pieces. He speaks primarily of his deeper understanding of the relationship between man and God. Buber begins by stating that "many an inexact, or indeed inaccurate, expression in the earlier addresses is clarified in the later ones, in correspondence with my own progress toward clarity."[107] He sees that there had been "a process of clarification" that took place during the years of these writings. He reflects that in this process "my words became clear to myself."[108]

Buber makes a concerted effort to repudiate views that are either directly attributable to his prior positions or are similar to these positions. First, he labels as "inexact" that statement "in the second address that 'this God' had emerged from the striving for unity" of man.[109] Buber goes on to say that "divine images originate not in the depths of a lonely soul."[110] In the "Preface" Buber rejects the idea that God is "the product of a semiartistic interpretation of the world"[111] and that He is something "created by, or developed within, man."[112]

Second, Buber insists on clarifying the concept of "the realization of God," that is, as put forth in one of his early essays, that "God must be transmuted from an abstract truth into reality."[113] Buber acknowledges that this concept "induces" the idea that "God is not, but that He becomes—either within man or within mankind."[114] Finally, he shows great concern to point out that the subjective dimensions of man's experience (*Erlebnis*) or experiencing are of no concern to him. Buber admits that he may have "contributed" to the "absolutizing" of the subjective experience as over against recognizing the reality of the Other who stands in relation to man.[115]

Buber emphasizes that God is a reality, a Thou, who addresses and stands as other to man. He is "not a metaphysical idea, nor a moral ideal, nor a projection of a psychic or social image, nor anything at all created by, or developed within, man."[116] Thus, God is *not* a dimension of human or interhuman existence. This affirmation brought Buber to also clarify his portrait of Judaism. Judaism is not just the product of man's urges and powers. Judaism reflects "something that takes place between man and God, that is, in the reality of their relationship, the mutual reality of God and man."[117]

Buber does not deny that man's reflections upon the encounter with God are influenced by many factors. The way that people have understood God does mirror the social and intellectual climate of the time, but this does not undermine the *fact* of the encounter itself. Man's ideas about God are the true "products of divine-human encounters, of man's attempt to grasp the inexplicable as and when it happens to him . . ."[118] Buber concludes by saying that "man does not possess God Himself, but he encounters God Himself."[119]

## II. The Philosophy of Dialogue

The following treatment of the book *I and Thou*[120] has two foci. First, there will be an examination of the central insights that generate Buber's portrait of the life of dialogue. Second, *I and Thou* will be analyzed in the context of the earlier writings by Buber that were explored previously. The continuities between Buber's previous positions and the presentation in *I and Thou* will be used as the point of departure for elaborating the threat to Buber's newly won understanding that arises out of the book itself. Insofar as the view of authentic living is haunted by ideas and images from the past, that is, from the "mystical" and "realization" periods, the message of the dialogical character of man's life with others and with God is undermined.

The goal of the following pages is not to question the importance and depth of Buber's dialogical philosophy. Rather, it is to continue to present a portrait of this man, Martin Buber, who struggled unceasingly to understand the meaning of being human. The resolution to this struggle did not come from an instantaneous flash of insight. As we have seen, Buber's probings into the meaning of life continued unabated for two decades before he wrote *I and Thou*. In the end, the solution comes about not by rejecting a significant part of his past, but by retaining aspects of previous positions. These aspects are reintegrated into a new whole by Buber's vision of man's life of dialogue. Man's encounters with other men and with God *is* powerfully affirmed by Buber, but ambiguities also remain. The tension between Buber's early thinking and his mature work will be illuminated in the following pages.

There is no doubt that Buber recognized *I and Thou* as the core of his mature understanding of the nature of authentic living. In it he bore witness, as he said, to a vision that had "afflicted me repeatedly since my youth but had always been dimmed again."[121] In *I and Thou* this vision finally "achieved a constant clarity."[122] All that followed the writing of this book was seen by him as mere "additions" and "clarifications."

Buber begins *I and Thou* by describing man as a relational being. Man cannot be known in isolation from the world, the human community, and God. To exist as a human being is to live in relation to others, and there are two ways of relating. As Buber writes, "There is no I as such but only the I of the basic word I-You and the I of the basic word I-It."[123] The I of him who says "You" or "Thou" to another lives in the most complete human way. To address another as "Thou" is to turn with one's whole being and to fully and openly listen and respond to the other. On the other hand, to turn and say "It" to another, or to treat another as an It, is to use the other as a means for one's own activity or goals. To say "It" is to refuse mutuality.

From the time of Buber's student years he was deeply impressed by the philosopher, Ludwig Feuerbach, who wrote that

> The *essence* of man is contained only in the community, in the *unity of man with man*—a unity, however, that rests on the *reality* of the *distinction* between "I" and "You."[124]

The relational character of man which is so briefly stated by Feuerbach, and which became a cornerstone in the thought of Marx, finds its fullest development in Buber's *I and Thou*. In the strongest possible way Buber maintained that to live is to live with others. "All actual life is encounter."[125]

The same thought is put in another way in the statement that "man becomes an I through a You."[126] It is through relation to others that man becomes fully human, that he becomes all that he can be. If relationships are spurned or only partially entered into, then something essential is missing. The person who can only say "It" is thus a terribly constricted being.

The term reciprocity best characterizes the relationship of an "I" to a "Thou." Buber writes that "relation is reciprocity," which means that "my You acts on me as I act on it."[127] The highest life is that which is frequently punctuated by encounters of this kind. During these encounters there is mutuality of action and response, of the active and the passive. Buber holds that at the time of the encounter both sides live fully in the present. Saying "Thou" to another brings one to live in a new realm, the between (*das Zwischen*). In this realm man discovers that distractions and factors from the past as well as hopes and fears for the future evaporate in the freedom of the present.[128]

In *I and Thou* language is the key to the true nature of man and the universe. For example, language reveals the relational character of man and the fact that there are two ways of relating. Although language is only fully manifest in the life of man with man, the insights from language guide Buber in grasping man's turning to non-human others. Man's life with the things of nature stands just below the threshold of language, but there is real encounter. Man's creative interaction with the realm of art is also beyond the exchange of spoken words, even though man often feels addressed and is capable of response.

Buber's understanding of the relationship between man and God, which is described in the third section of *I and Thou,* is built upon the supposition that "the relation to a human being is the proper metaphor for the relation to God—as genuine address is here accorded a genuine answer."[129] The metaphor of relationship implies that God is both distinct from and related to man. God is distinct in the sense that He is not the creation of man or a mere dimension of the human or interhuman realm. Likewise, He is not a part or product of nature. God is a being who, though distinct, is not aloof from man. Buber rejects the deist Creator and the philosopher's Unmoved Mover. Both of these conceptions of God are hypotheses that reason arrives at because of some evidence in the world. However, the belief that God relates to man, that is, addresses and responds to man, is not based on a logical inference but on an experienced event.

The event of revelation transforms the individual who participates in it. He knows that something has occurred and that the "more" that he now has cannot be taken away. Although no explanations are adequate to the dynamics and meaning of revelation, Buber delineates, in the section on revelation, three elements in the totality of this event.[130] The individual is aware, first, that someone is present and concerned, that is, that a meeting has taken place. Second, there is "the inexpressible confirmation of meaning." One does not come away with a content or piece of knowledge that can be made into a shield or slogan. Yet, out of the meeting there is the awareness that life in its totality, and the individual's life in particular, is meaningful.

The dialogue with God brings forth the realization that the universe is ruled neither by chaos nor by a fickle Zeus. There is an Other, and He seeks and finds man. Third, this meaning "wants to be demonstrated by us in this life and this world." The relationship to God does not bring man out of the world. Rather, it thrusts man into the world in the deepest way.

Buber affirms that "all revelation is a calling and a mission."[131] The person who lives before God finds that at every moment there is a task to be done. Buber holds that man's life in the world is the verification of the encounters with God. Man's response to the divine address must be lived out. This understanding of "calling and mission" stands in greatest contrast to those who seek to divorce the religious life from man's life with others.

In describing the relationship between man and God, Buber does not shun the idea of mutuality that is so clearly apparent in the dialogue between man and man. While many philosophers of religion have been scandalized by the idea of mutuality in the divine-human encounter, Buber confidently asserts: "That you need God more than anything, you know at all times in your heart. But don't you know also that God needs you—in the fullness of his eternity, you?"[132] Man's share of this mutuality is expressed, as we have seen, in his living out the particular task that God has for him.

Buber held that *I and Thou* stood diametrically opposed to all mysticism. Mysticism is defined in the book as the experience of unity in which the awareness of duality disappears.[133] While a general critique of mystic doctrines is woven throughout the book, the opposition to mysticism becomes fully manifest in a number of powerful passages. The first of these is in connection with what is described as a "waking dream" (*Wachtraum*).[134] This "waking dream" is discussed at the end of the second of three sections in *I and Thou*. The second section paints a depressing picture of the decline of the life of dialogue and the growth of the I-It dimension in the modern world. In the face of the ever-growing "It" world, people often are forced to look at themselves and their lives. This act of self-examination commences with the feeling that the "I" or self is sick. The individual knows that the world of "It," of utility and exploitation, does not exhaust the possibilities of existence; and a frantic search for the "real" henceforth ensues. Buber affirms that the individual in this situation is vaguely aware of the solution for his frightening alienation. The individual must turn to the world and to others with the "Thou" of address. However, this awareness of the right path is often ignored. People insist on allowing reason to find the way out. Reason then attempts to overcome alienation, not by requiring a fundamental change in life (*teshuvah*), but by suggesting that the alienation is only an illusion.

Reason endeavors to remedy the alienation between the self and the world in one of two ways. These two are the customary paths of mysticism. In the first case, reason tries to erase alienation by suggesting that there is no disharmony between the universe and the soul, because, ultimately, everything is a part of that totality which is the universe. The "I is contained in the world." The self is really an aspect of the "One and All" of the universe, and thus the separation between the self and the outside world is itself only a dream. On the other hand, thought may paint a different picture, that is, offer a different variety of mysticism's reductionism. In this case the soul is proclaimed as the "One and All" and the "world is contained in the I." Buber concludes this discussion or story by saying that the horror of alienation is not overcome by these false remedies. Eventually the individual, when he sees "in a flash" both false portraits of the world side by side, is "seized by a deeper horror." This is the final statement in the second section of *I and Thou* and it points to the third section, where the portrait of the "I" and "Thou" between man and God is presented.

The longest distinct segment in *I and Thou* is devoted to a lengthy treatment of mysticism.[135] In this segment Buber admits that he had at one time also interpreted certain occurrences as experiences of mystic unity. Buber's rejection of the mystic's view of the nature of man, world, and God has a strength and clarity about it that surely reflects an understanding that Buber has gradually arrived at over the years.

Buber again describes two basic varieties of mysticism. In the

## 74  What Does Revelation Mean for the Modern Jew?

first the self is swallowed up by the other, that is, by God. This is accomplished either by the individual freeing himself from his distinctiveness as a person—becoming "freed of I-hood"—or by merging the self with God. Often ecstasy is the means for this unification of man and God. Buber takes Meister Eckhart's belief that "God begets [Christ] eternally in the human soul"[136] as the paradigm of this view.

The second variety of mysticism also collapses one side of the I-Thou relation into the other. Here the outcome is not the "All" of God, but the "coronation of the self."[137] The identity of the human and the divine is posited as the ultimate truth that lies hidden behind the everyday world. The task of man is to come to the recognition of the true nature of the self. The treatment of the self in the *Upanishads* is used by Buber to illustrate this mystic variety.

Buber, of course, sees these mystical views as erroneous, because they deny the reality of the I-Thou relationship. At a crucial point in this discussion of mysticism an important question is introduced, a question that Buber seems to feel compelled to confront.[138] An interlocutor queries: "Have we any right to doubt the faithfulness of this testimony?"—this testimony about the ultimate unity of man and God. Buber, who investigated such testimonies in *Ecstatic Confessions* and other writings, replies that there are two events which have led many to believe in mystical doctrines of unity. Buber goes on to offer alternate interpretations to these events.

First, there is the event in which "the soul may become one."[139] Here the individual turns away from the world and tries to compose the self. There are moments, according to Buber, when the individual must look into the self and not be distracted by anything outside. Although he acknowledges the importance of these moments, Buber holds that the decisive question is whether these moments are to be understood as the goal of life or as the means toward something higher. Many mystics see this becoming united of the self as the highest experience and they cultivate such moments in order to "savor the bliss" of unity. In Buber's view these moments are waystations or times of preparation for the next series of encounters. Those who refuse to return from this experience of the self's unity have rejected the "supreme duty" of enriching the world.

The second experience that can be mistaken for an experience of unification often arises at the moment of encounter between the individual and the other. At times the individual is so overcome by the ecstasy of encounter that consciousness of a distinct "I" and a distinct "Thou" is momentarily lost. In Buber's words,

> What the ecstatic calls unification is the rapturous dynamics of the relationship . . . the relationship itself in its vital unity is felt so vehemently that its members pale in the process . . .[140]

In the above two ways Buber seeks to account for mystical testimonies about unification. He sees them as either the experience of the concentration of the self into a unity or as the rapturous ecstasy of the individual who momentarily loses awareness of the two sides of the encounter with the other.

In the same treatment of mysticism Buber offers a number of reasons that mitigate against the truth of the various doctrines of immersion of the "All" into the self. He finds that such doctrines denigrate both the integrity of the person and the vitality of the world. These doctrines demand that the self be stripped of emotions, sensuousness, and instincts in order to be purified. However, Buber affirms that the "abstract man" who remains is not fully a person. Only through the life of dialogue does man become all that he can be. Additionally, in rejecting the everyday world as illusory, the mystic gives away that which he is entrusted to help perfect. Buber refuses to recognize the mystic's state of "deep sleep" as the highest goal of life, when there is a beckoning world to be addressed and redeemed.

In the end, says Buber, we cannot know the ultimate truth nor what lies beyond our death. Yet, we should not repudiate that which we can know about, in order to anticipate death. In this life there is no unity of God and man. The ecstatics who give up the self and those who deny the world are mistaken. Man does not know the ultimate nature of God, but he can and does encounter Him. In the concluding paragraph of this discussion,

Buber writes: "God embraces but is not the universe; just so, God embraces but is not my self."[141]

## The Tensions Within *I and Thou*

The focal point of the last section of this chapter is the contention that *I and Thou* is not fully satisfactory in breaking with Buber's past standpoints. There are elements in this book that undermine its clarity as a statement about the reality of the dialogue between God and man. These elements, not surprisingly, have strong affinities with some of Buber's earlier work. Buber's earlier views are manifested not in blatant statements of an ecstatic or immanental stamp, but in descriptions of I and Thou encounters in which there is no real encounter. The reciprocity or mutuality of the meeting between the two partners, which is a vital characteristic of true encounters, disappears in some of Buber's descriptions of man's "dialogue" with animate and inanimate objects of nature and with God.

That there are lines of continuity between the earlier works and *I and Thou* has been acknowledged by Buber and endlessly pointed out by his critics. Maurice Friedman's conclusions about these lines of continuity exemplify the observations of most critics:

> Most of the ideas which appear in the early periods are not really discarded in the latter but are preserved in changed form. Thus Buber's existentialism [his ideas on realization] retains much of his mysticism, and his dialogical philosophy in turn includes important mystical and existential elements.[142]

However, Buber's commentators do not usually recognize that those mystical and "existentialist" strands in *I and Thou* pose a grave threat to the philosophy of dialogue. Dialogue demands two distinct partners who turn in mutuality to one another, while, as we have seen, the separation between the participants as well as the mutuality of the encounter were not hallmarks of Buber's previous positions. In the mystical stage God entered into and took over the human soul by means of the ecstatic experience. According to the writings on realization, God was created through man's establishment of the hidden unity of all things.

Buber was aware of the tensions between his earlier and later thought. It may well be for this reason that he tried to minimize the radical nature of his first writings. Statements of a mystic or ecstatic coloring were sometimes changed or removed by Buber when his early writings were later reprinted.[143] In the "Preface" to the 1923 edition of his *Addresses on Judaism* Buber insisted that some of his statements about God's realization were inexact or had been misunderstood, despite the more obvious explanation that he had changed his views about the relationship between God and man over the decade. Finally, Buber mitigated the conflict between his different standpoints by including very few pieces written before 1919 in his three-volume collected works.[144]

The omnipresence of Buber's hostility toward mysticism in *I and Thou* underscores the opposition that he saw between mysticism and dialogue. He was compelled to attack this religious phenomenon, given the definition of mysticism that he utilized: the experience of unity where there is no longer an awareness of duality.[145] One of the most insightful critics of modern Jewish thought, Emil Fackenheim, also saw this irreconcilability of mysticism and dialogue. In his essay, "Martin Buber's Concept of Revelation," Fackenheim maintained that, from the standpoint of dialogue, mysticism is "a form of pseudo-religion," because "it denies either the reality of all meeting, or else at least that the supreme moment is a moment of meeting."[146] Fackenheim ignores the mystic strands in *I and Thou,* implying that given the conflict between mysticism and dialogue, the former must have been firmly rejected by Buber in his great work.

The presence of elements in *I and Thou* that threaten the reality of a mutual relationship between two partners is clearest in connection with Buber's descriptions of encounters outside the human realm. These are also the places in his book that show the strongest affinities with his earlier writings. First, Buber speaks of man's dialogue with "spiritual beings" and he clearly intends by this to point to the realm of art.[147] He describes the "dialogue" between the artist and his work and between the "receptive beholder" and the artistic creation.[148] This treatment of art is in harmony with his discussions of the artist and the experience of art in his earlier writings. Still, one can raise doubts about the success of this attempt to integrate into his philosophy of dialogue these earlier interests and experiences. Further, these doubts are strongly reinforced when we focus on Buber's treatment of the realm of nature.

Second, throughout the whole gamut of his authorship, Buber has given great significance to experiences of nature, which he once called "this huge sphere that reaches from the stones to the stars."[149] While there are no particular difficulties in interpreting these experiences in ecstatic terms or in accordance with his theory of "realization," inescapable questions arise when he attempts to describe his *meetings* with these natural things. As long as the dialogue between persons is the great metaphor for all I-Thou meetings, the mutuality of the encounter and the separateness of the two sides of the relationship are beyond doubt. Yet, when the discussion turns to the realm of nature, especially to inanimate objects, the reciprocity of the encounter is blurred or even dissipated. Despite Buber's protests to the contrary, it is extremely difficult to imagine what "reciprocity" means in the context of relationship between a person and a piece of rock. One suspects, at the least, that there is a projection from the human side onto the object, and that this projection is then interpreted as response coming from the other side.[150]

In particular, Buber's descriptions of the I-Thou meetings with the realm of nature have important ramifications for our assessment of his understanding of the relationship between man and God. Again, as long as the dialogue between persons is the great metaphor for the relationship between man and God, the fact of mutuality or reciprocity is assured. However, if man's meeting with a tree or rock is an important example of the I-Thou relation, may not the encounter with God resemble this meeting more than the meeting between man and man? Stated in another way, if there are I-Thou meetings with rocks, can one be certain that the dialogue with God is more than just the monologue of man with his own projection? In light of the various experiences that are allowed to count as I-Thou meetings, the understanding of God in *I and Thou* no longer appears as a radical break with the past.

There are three examples of descriptions of experiences with nature that can be traced through Buber's writings on mysticism, realization, and dialogue.[151] The similarities in the ways Buber describes these experiences are striking, despite the differing interpretations that are offered. These interpretations vary according to the particular philosophical standpoint of the time. Buber's descriptions of his experiences of a tree, a piece of mica, and a cat, make evident the difficulty that these experiences pose for the philosophy of dialogue.

Buber has often spoken of an experience of a tree. In the essay "On Jacob Boehme" he offers what one critic terms a "personal confession."[152] Buber comments on the mystical vision that finds "heaven and earth with all being, and even God himself, reside in man!"

> This marvelous world-feeling has become peculiarly our own. We have woven it into our innermost experience . . . And we are sometimes overcome with a desire to put our arms around a young tree and feel the same life-rhythm that pulsates in us . . .[153]

This confession is followed by examples of other things that occur in nature and that can be understood as our own inner events. In Buber's most important statement of realization, *Daniel,* we find another experience of a tree:

> With all your directed power, receive the tree, surrender yourself to it. Until you feel its bark as your skin and the springing forth of a branch from the trunk like the striving in your muscles . . . But also in the transformation your direction is with you, and through it you experience the tree so that you attain in it to the unity.[154]

*I and Thou* also includes a statement about a tree. In fact, the description has an important place in the book, since it comes as the first example of the I-It and the I-Thou relationships.

> I contemplate a tree.
> I can accept it as a picture . . .
> I can feel it as movement: the flowing veins around the sturdy, striving core . . .
>
> But it can also happen, if will and grace are joined, that as I contemplate the tree I am drawn into a relation, and the tree ceases to be an It. The power of exclusiveness has seized me.[155]

The example of gazing at a rock, or, in particular, at a piece of mica, cuts across the three periods of Buber's writings. In *Ecstatic Confessions* Buber describes the experience of unity that came through looking at a heap of stones. Maurice Friedman summarized Buber's exclamation in this way:

> One is no longer aware of looking at a rock, one experiences only unity, the world: oneself. All forces are united and felt as unity, and in the middle of them lives and shines the stone which is contemplated. The soul experiences the unity of the 'I,' and in it the unity of 'I' and the world, no longer a content but that which is infinitely more than all content.[156]

At another pivotal place, this time in the concluding chapter "On Unity" in *Daniel,* Buber writes of picking up a piece of mica. He says that at first awareness of a distinct object and subject left him, but when he again looked at the mica the feeling of unity too was gone. Yet, more importantly,

> there it burned in me as though to create. I closed my eyes, I gathered in my strength, I bound myself with my object, I raised the mica into the kingdom of the existing. And there . . . I first felt: *I,* there I first was I.[157]

In *I and Thou* Buber refers to the same experience of picking up the piece of mica, but again his interpretation has changed. He now understands this experience as a fleeting meeting, at which what at one moment is addressed as a "Thou" quickly recedes into the world of "It":

> O fragment of mica, it was while contemplating you that I first understood that I is not something 'in me' . . . But when something does emerge from among things, something living, and becomes a being for me, and comes to me, near and eloquent, how unavoidably briefly it is for me nothing but You![158]

The encounter with a "dumb animal," or a cat in particular, is found in a number of Buber's works. In the essay on Boehme, Buber uses the example of seeing a "dumb animal" to indicate the way man learns about himself. He writes that we "read in the eyes of a dumb animal our very own secret."[159] In a much longer treatment in *I and Thou* we find:

> The eyes of an animal have the capacity of a great language . . .
> I sometimes look into the eyes of a house cat . . . Undeniably, this cat began its glance by asking me with a glance that was ignited by the breath of my glance: "Can it be that you mean me? Do you actually want that I should not merely do tricks for you? Do I concern you? Am I there for you? . . ."[160]

The preceding excerpts are more than just interesting examples of personal experiences that are used again and again in connection with different interpretations. There is certainly nothing wrong with reinterpreting experiences in light of new understandings. This harmless fact of reinterpretation is what most commentators find in these parallel descriptions about trees, rocks, and animals.[161] However, as indicated previously, while there are no necessary philosophical problems in interpreting these experiences in terms of mysticism or realization, they are very problematic for the philosophy of *I and Thou*.

Responding to criticism about the above I-Thou encounters, Buber added an "Afterword" to *I and Thou* in 1957.[162] He refused to concede that experiences of nature were not I-Thou encounters, although he had great difficulty in indicating their character of mutuality or reciprocity. Buber insisted that these occurrences were not "mystical."[163] He even appealed to his readers to overturn their accustomed patterns of thought in trying to understand the dimension of mutuality in connection with "this huge sphere that reaches from the stones to the stars."[164]

One of Buber's long-time critics, and certainly not his most sympathetic one, Gershom Scholem, also noted the problematic nature of these descriptions for the philosophy of dialogue. In the essay, "Martin Buber's Conception of Judaism," Scholem contended that from his earliest writings Buber was fascinated and captivated by the "cult" of *Erlebnis*.[165] Scholem meant by this that Buber cultivated and valued dynamic, quasi-mystical and quasi-ecstatic experience above everything else. Scholem claimed to find this cult of living experience and the goal of mystical vision in all periods of Buber's authorship. In arguing that Buber's ever-present mysticism[166] undermined his philosophy of dialogue, Scholem referred to the descriptions of experiences with a tree and a cat. He wrote,

> His "empirical" descriptions of his own concrete I-Thou experiences, such as his contemplation of a tree or his gazing into the eyes of his pet cat, are, it seems to me, to be understood as nothing other than descriptions of mystical experiences.[167]

While Scholem goes too far in seeing Buber's I-Thou philosophy as essentially a "slogan" that covers over his mysticism,[168] there is some force to Scholem's contentions. Although Buber's powerful refutations of mysticism in *I and Thou* are certainly to be taken seriously, in retaining elements from his earlier works, the clarity of his dialogical philosophy is obscured. Once again, if the encounter with nature is taken as exemplifying the mutuality of the I-Thou relationship, can we be certain that the dialogue between man and God is not merely a monologue of man with himself?

When we examine specific statements in *I and Thou* about man's relationship to God, our lingering questions about

Buber's break with his past positions remain. Some critics have opined that in *I and Thou* God is essentially seen as a dimension of the world. While the crude charge of pantheism is out of place,[169] there is reason to be confused about this point. Buber writes, for example, "Although we on earth never behold God without world but only the world in God, by beholding we eternally form God's form."[170] He also writes, "Looking away from the world is no help toward God; staring at the world is no help either; but whoever beholds the world in him stands in his presence."[171] These lines are clearly reminiscent of earlier statements by Buber to the effect that God is discovered or realized in turning to the world. One searches vainly throughout *I and Thou* to find a detailed statement about the direct relationship to God, in which man stands alone with Him.[172]

It might be supposed that these matters are clarified in the one lengthy section of *I and Thou* in which revelation is discussed.[173] This is not the case. Buber's description is very enigmatic. First, Buber begins and concludes this section on revelation by saying that there is the "primal phenomenon" or "eternal revelation," which is "present in the here and now."[174] The reader is left to surmise that there are no distinct acts in which God turns toward man. There is just one eternal addressing from God's side. Second, Buber's general conviction that words are inadequate in describing this event leads to problematic statements about that which is addressing man and about the content of such addressing. The recipient of revelation is "unable to indicate what that is like with which one is associated." One comes away with no specific content, that is, there is no "formula or image" for it. Third, in describing man's acceptance of being turned to, he refers to Nietzsche. He quotes Nietzsche's statement: "one accepts, one does not ask who gives." Despite the accompanying affirmation that Nietzsche is "faithful to actuality in his report," the reference to Nietzsche only intensifies the fear that there is nothing really addressing man. Finally, towards the end of this segment Buber describes man's living before God in terms of living in the presence of mystery:

84  What Does Revelation Mean for the Modern Jew?

> That before which we live, that in which we live, that out of which and into which we live, the mystery—has remained what it was. It has become present for us, and through its presence it has made itself known to us as salvation; we have "known" it, but we have no knowledge of it that might diminish or extenuate its mysteriousness. We have come close to God, but no closer to an unriddling, unveiling of being . . .[175]

Too much is said if one concludes that, under scrutiny, the divine presence that Buber speaks of in *I and Thou* eventually dissolves into the world, or into a formless mystery. Buber is as much, or more, a poet than a philosopher. He struggled to give words to experiences and insights that remained elusive. It is appropriate at this time to recall Buber's statement about his struggles to fathom and report about his life-experiences:

> Since I have matured to a life from my own experience . . . I have stood under the duty to insert the framework of the decisive experiences that I had at that time into the human inheritance of thought, but not as "my" experiences, rather as an insight valid and important for others and even for other kinds of men.[176]

Buber searched many years for the right words with which to understand and to speak of the relationship between the divine and the human. He eventually recognized that it was illegitimate to view God as "coming to birth in the human soul" or as that which must be created or "realized" in the world. He found that the philosophy of dialogue, in which the relationship between man and man is the great metaphor for the relationship between man and God, provided him with a satisfactory framework. Yet, as we have seen, there are dimensions of his experiences that refuse to be confined to the framework of that philosophy. Even the metaphor of dialogue left some things out. Buber was aware of the difficulties here, but he refused to manufacture a simple answer. The struggle for clarity continued. This is evidenced, among many other things, by the fact that Buber continued to rework *I and Thou* as late as the 1957 edition. Still, it is just to conclude that Buber came to no *fully* satisfactory solution. *I and Thou* stands as an eloquent, if sometimes fragmentary solution; a testimony to Buber's persistent struggles.

Chapter IV
# Emil Fackenheim:
# The New "Vulnerability" to History

Emil Fackenheim's writings of the past fifteen years reflect his passionate struggle with the problem of the meaning of history. Once again, we come upon a man who is *compelled* to wrestle with a problem, rather than a thinker who comes upon a question. There is an overpowering intensity to these writings. For Fackenheim, serenity and philosophic distance are nothing less than deceptive temptations when the future existence of the Jewish people is at stake. He believes that the power and quality of Jewish existence is being thoroughly tested by the events of modern history. In the book *The Jewish Return Into History,* he writes:

> Philosophical and religious thought widely take themselves to be immune and indeed indifferent to the "accidents" of "mere" history. The conscious repudiation of this view, first in abstracto and subsequently in relation to the events of our age, is the major change in my thinking . . . Thought, or at any rate Jewish thought, shows its strength precisely by making itself vulnerable . . . The vulnerability is to the stern challenge of epoch-making events. Thus it was at the beginning of Jewish history. Thus it remains—or has once again become—in our time.[1]

Fackenheim's appreciation of the radical challenge of history distinguishes his latest work from his works written before 1967. In particular, the effort to forge a meaningful response to the unimaginable evil of the Holocaust characterizes the dramatic transformation in Fackenheim's theological development.

Despite the ongoing controversy that surrounds much of Fackenheim's later thought, his new focus is neither fortuitous nor the outcome of some idiosyncratic moods. The change is not fortuitous, because it rests upon Fackenheim's carefully enunciated philosophic dissatisfaction with his earlier positions. The transformation is not idiosyncratic, because his diagnosis of the errors and lacunae of his prior standpoints is also a penetrating critique of many modern theological stances. The confrontation with the Holocaust crystallized Fackenheim's doubts about the foundations of his theological reflections and led him to explore areas that have been neglected by many before him. The existential necessity of an open, "vulnerable," encounter with history became unescapable as he recognized the threat that the Holocaust continued to pose to the religious foundations of Jewish life.

Emil Fackenheim was born in Halle, Germany, in 1916. He was ordained as a rabbi at the *Hochschule für die Wissenschaft des Judentums* in Berlin in 1939. Before his ordination, in 1938 as a youth of 22, he was arrested and sent to the protoconcentration camp of Sachsenhausen. This experience, which undoubtedly left a severe impression on Fackenheim, lay submerged in his mind for decades. It was only in 1975, after already speaking of the Holocaust for over eight years, that he was able to publicly confront this experience.[2] In 1940 he went to Canada and eventually became a member of the department of philosophy at the University of Toronto.

## I. Fackenheim's Early Theological Positions

Fackenheim's first theological position is best seen in his essay of 1954, "An Outline of Modern Jewish Theology."[3] The essay offers guidelines for future efforts at working out a systematic theology for the modern Jew. The cardinal point of his position is stated as follows:

> Modern theology must "work its way up," i.e., show, by an analysis of the human condition, that man's existence, properly understood, forces him to raise the question of the Supernatural, and the existential problem of the "leap into faith," . . . *From this it follows that the analysis of the human condition constitutes the necessary prolegomenon for all modern Jewish and, indeed, all modern theology.*[4]

In addition to this task of explaining "the faith by which the Jew lives insofar as he is a man," the Jewish theologian must also illuminate "the faith by which the Jew lives insofar as he is a Jew; this faith, involving the nature and destiny of Israel before God."[5]

The treatment of the human condition that is the core of Fackenheim's earliest method accentuates the tensions that pervade existence. The writings prior to 1957 examine what he terms the "contradictions" in man (natural needs/moral and spiritual nature), in history (moral progress/tragic frustration), and in moral life (the tension between "is" and "ought").[6] In all of these fundamental areas of human experience the individual is faced with dilemmas. Further, these particular dilemmas underscore the seemingly tragic nature of life itself. Fackenheim characterizes the human responses to this situation in two ways. First, there are those who valiantly struggle with these contradictions, but who are ultimately unable to go further than the recognition of the tragedy of human existence.[7] On the other hand, faith asserts "that what is contradictory to finite understanding is yet ultimately not contradictory."[8] The religious man does not turn from life and its dilemmas, but is able to see that they are "resolved" by God, the Creator and Redeemer of all. Beginning with a portrait of the human condition, Fackenheim is thus able to conclude that faith is the "positive answer, given by way of personal commitment, to existential questions of ultimate significance."[9]

The remaining task of the Jewish theologian, the faith "involving the nature and destiny of Israel before God," is discussed by Fackenheim in terms of the Jew's response to God's revelations in the past. What distinguishes the Jew from the Muslim or Christian, Fackenheim suggests, is his belief in the "actuality" of specific divine revelations and his lived response to the covenant which is founded on these events. As Fackenheim writes, "The God-man relation demands of the Jew . . . a response expressing his Jewishness in all its particularity. This response is Halachah."[10] Fackenheim has thus explained the uniqueness of Jewish faith by looking into God's revelations to the Jewish community in the past and by describing the on-going role of Halacha as the Jew's live-out response to God's call.

Fackenheim is neither alone nor first in seeing that "the analysis of the human condition constitutes the necessary prolegomenon for all . . . modern theology."[11] His thinking is in harmony with the powerful anthropological thrust which is characteristic of religious thought from the time of René Descartes. Descartes' famous formula "cogito ergo sum," found in the *Discourse on Method* of 1637, is universally acclaimed as the beginning of modern philosophy. Religious reflection has been equally indebted to the "cogito," since religious thinkers after Descartes have customarily begun their discussions about the nature and origin of religion as well as man's relationship to God with statements about man's consciousness, reason, moral life, feelings, or situation in the world.

A brief examination of some of the modern religious thinkers who have used man's situation in the world, or the human condition, as the starting point for their reflections, will make the significance of Fackenheim's later refutations of this position more evident. A complex example can be isolated in the writings of the nineteenth century Danish philosopher, Soren Kierkegaard. Kierkegaard writes *The Sickness Unto Death,* under the pseudonym Anti-Climacus,[12] in which all of the types or stages of human existence are portrayed. Anti-Climacus argues that man is a synthesis of "the infinite and the finite," a synthesis that is neither "constituted," i.e., completed, at birth nor through any of man's struggles to find inner harmony. In light of this, all of the "human" stages or types of life are riddled by despair. The resolution and antithesis of despair, "faith," comes only when man is made anew by God. Thus, for Anti-Climacus the analysis of the human condition is the foundation upon which the necessity of the despairing leap of faith is demonstrated.

Christian and Jewish philosophers of religion in the present century have often relied upon an analysis of the human condition to provide a foundation for their arguments about the necessity of faith. Paul Tillich stands as an obvious parallel to Fackenheim's earliest position. Tillich spoke of the "method of correlation," whereby problems which arise from the human situation are provided an answer through revelation. Fackenheim's standpoint was influenced by his Jewish predecessors, Franz Rosenzweig and Martin Buber. Rosenzweig commences *The Star of Redemption* with a depiction of man's fear of death. Rosenzweig held that the fear of death is omnipresent, unavoidable, and uniquely diagnostic of human existence. He concludes his work by stating that death cannot be escaped, but that the religious life enables the individual to achieve authenticity by both facing death and fearlessly living in the world.[13] Similarly, Martin Buber demonstrated, in *I and Thou,* the necessity of man's relationship to God by describing man's twofold nature. Buber states that man is fundamentally a relational being and that there are two ways of relating to others. Man turns to others with the "It" of utilization or the "Thou" of address. While Buber does not condemn the necessity of at times saying "It," he affirms that human existence cannot be complete unless the individual addresses others, and, especially, the "eternal Thou."

The first change in Fackenheim's theological stance, which came in 1957, is chronicled in an essay of 1967, "These Twenty Years: A Reappraisal."[14] This essay appears as the "Introduction" to a group of collected essays, *Quest for Past and Future,* and in it Fackenheim delineates the reasons that brought him, ten years earlier, to repudiate elements in his first position.

On the one hand, Fackenheim discovered that there were inherent faults in the method of demonstrating the necessity of faith by analyzing the human condition. He was suspicious of this method because it assumed that the portrait of the human condition which it introduced was a portrait that was as acceptable to unbelievers and to philosophers as it was to theologians. However, it was clear that the understanding of man which theologians spoke of was weighted from the start in the direction of the believer's hoped-for conclusion.[15] The method was thus problematic, because it attributed to "unbelief questions which are asked—as well as answered—only by belief." Fackenheim also realized that it was incorrect to "set up alternatives of faith and despair" for, in his words, "there is both despair within faith and serene confidence without it."[16]

On the other hand, Fackenheim rejected his prior theological stance because it failed to do justice to *Jewish* belief. Fackenheim's earliest treatment of Jewish belief accentuated the importance of the Jew's openness to God's voice as it was manifested in past events. He now rejected this understanding, because it turned faith into a static thing by closing off the possibility of God's voice in the present. Jewish life must not be guarded from the "radical surprise" of discovering God's revelation in the present.[17] Fackenheim concluded, additionally, that his previous misunderstandings were results of his failure to stand "within Jewish faith" when addressing religious and philosophical issues. He recognized that it was a type of self-deception for the Jewish thinker to believe that he could address the great problems of contemporary life by first abstracting himself out of the ongoing covenant between God and the Jewish people.

Two dimensions of this second stage of Fackenheim's theological development are best expressed in the definition of his new stance, "committed openness to the voice of God."[18] Jewish theology is possible only after there has been a commitment to Jewish existence. The commitment, in turn, leads to an openness to God's voice in the present as well as in the past. In referring to the "singled-out condition" of the Jew, Fackenheim touches upon a basic element of traditional Jewish self-understanding which is expressed by the term "election." Fackenheim saw that Jewish belief does not originate out of man's quest for God or out of some abstract relationship between God and man. The relationship, the covenant, between God and Israel, began with God's election of this particular people, and Fackenheim reiterates the importance of election by making the Jew's "singled-out condition" *the* point of departure for modern Jewish theology.

Thus, the second stage is a departure from the first, because it insists that authentically Jewish thought arises out of a commitment to revelation in the past and an openness to its possibility for the future. However, an analysis of the essays of the nine or ten years during which he held this view, and before his profound wrestling with the meaning of the Holocaust, indicates that there is both restlessness and a continual development during this stage. In this sense, the stage is best understood as a transitional period, rather than a time when he has a consistent, permanent stance. A number of problems are struggled with and themes discussed and rediscussed until we find a solution in the third stage, that is, the treatment of the Holocaust.

What is omnipresent in these essays is the idea that the Jew cannot stand *between* faith and the rejection of faith. The Jewish theologian must recognize that he speaks out of a standpoint of belief. He must also recognize that the secularist and the philosopher *qua* philosopher is also committed to a stance, of unbelief, before he speaks. Fackenheim writes that "I hold the affirmation of revelation to presuppose a commitment, which in turn permeates the religious thinking which springs from it."[19]

Fackenheim's understanding of the "singled-out" quality of Jewish existence does undergo change during this period. In the first stage of his work, he spoke of the individual possibly being singled out through revelation.[20] The first essays of the new stage describe this dimension of Jewish existence in terms of the community, but the singling-out is by other humans in history. Thus, we find Fackenheim suggesting that other critics have pointed to the Jews' tenacious will to survive in order to express the view that the Jewish group, like other groups, "may cling defiantly to the very trait which singles them out."[21] A few years later Fackenheim writes that our age is "an age which has singled the Jew out with unprecedented grimness."[22] By 1965, Fackenheim describes God as singling out the Jewish people, at least through a prophetic message.[23] It is only when Fackenheim turns with utmost seriousness to the Holocaust, that he speaks of the radical religious significance of being singled out by God as a people in history.

There is an intense searching in Fackenheim's writings between the years 1964 and 1966. While there are references to the Holocaust throughout the second stage, the references become more frequent and more central. At the end of this period he affirms, for the first time, that the Jews may not think about religion without reflecting on Auschwitz.[24]

The essay of 1964, "On the Eclipse of God," indicates that Fackenheim has begun to see that the Holocaust raises a real challenge to Jewish belief. He writes, on the one hand, that "religious faith can be, and is, empirically verifiable; but nothing empirical can possibly refute it,"[25] and that the catastrophies or tragedies of our age only "test" faith. When faith emerges from such tests, "it both clarifies its own meaning and conquers tragedy."[26] On the other hand, Fackenheim ends this essay by both affirming the adequacy of Martin Buber's view that there are times when man experiences an eclipse of God and also, possibly, searching for something more.

> The Psalmist *in extremis* could rest in the irrefutability of faith. The modern believer *in extremis* must endure the full impact of its being undemonstrable as well; he must suffer the knowledge that to the world around him the concealed God is a non-existent God, and that he himself can do no more than testify to the contrary.[27]

The years between 1964 and 1966 witness an increasing amount of attention to the problem of the meaning of history, the possibility of God's radical incursion into history, and to Jewish testimony to God in the present.[28] In all, the problem of somehow bringing together God's Presence and the event of the Holocaust is expressed, in a variety of fragmentary forms, again and again in his writings.

> Such has been the contemporary Jew's experience with a secularism become deified, all-encompassing, demonic and mad. A Jew can hardly bear to transform this experience into testimony.[29]

> Is there an authentic Jewish enduring of the contradictions of present Jewish existence? Is it giving rise to a quest, to a listening, indeed, to an interrogating of God which, born of faith, may itself bespeak a Presence while as yet no voice is heard?[30]

> And is not . . . the Jew of the generation of Auschwitz required to do what, since Abraham, Jeremiah, and Job, Jews have always done in times of darkness—contend with the silent God, and bear witness to Him by this very contention?[31]

The great turning point, and the third stage, in Fackenheim's work commences when he finds that the Jew can finally bear to testify, bespeak a Presence, and even to powerfully witness to God's voice:

> Not until I faced this scandal [of Auschwitz] did I make what to me was, and still is, a momentous discovery. Jews throughout the world—rich and poor, learned and ignorant, believer and unbeliever—were already responding to Auschwitz, and in some measure had been doing so all along. Faced with the radical threat of extinction, they were stubbornly defying it, committing themselves, if to nothing more, to the survival of themselves and their children as Jews.[32]

It is not clear whether it is possible to point to a particular moment when Fackenheim first faced this "scandal." In a private conversation with this author he suggested that the turning point came at a conference between Jews and Christians held sometime in late 1966 or early 1967. All of his work that is published in 1967 takes the Holocaust as its point of departure and thus the leap from the second to the third stage undoubtedly occurred towards the end of 1966 or very early in 1967.[33] Even if it is possible to isolate a single moment of discovery, the discovery cannot be attributed to something entirely new that overpowered him, but to a coming together of problems and insights that had preoccupied him for these last years.

Finally, although there are thus three stages in the development of Fackenheim's thought including his most recent work of 1982, *To Mend the World,* it is important to recognize the differences in the relationships between the stages. While the second stage clearly stands as a repudiation of some of the fundamental views of the first, the third is a development, or better, a leap from the second, but a leap where no repudiation was necessary.

## II. The Confrontation with the Holocaust

Our endeavor to understand Fackenheim's new "vulnerability" to history requires two additional steps. First, we will unravel Fackenheim's view that the Holocaust and the establishing of the State of Israel are the most recent acts in the drama between God and Israel. Second, we will briefly discuss the main themes in his most recent work, as these indicate Fackenheim's continuing confrontation with the problem of the meaning of the Holocaust, a confrontation which now spans almost two decades.

In discussing the Holocaust, Fackenheim distinguishes the attempt to "explain" it from the quest for a genuine response to it. He characterizes the first type of effort as "blasphemous." Those who seek to explain the Holocaust believe that they can fully grasp it in one of the usual theological meaning-schemes such as "sin and punishment" or "chastisements of love." Fackenheim does not believe that such solutions really take seriously the horror of the event, and he even wonders whether God Himself will be able to put this event into a fully meaningful context.

Fackenheim is aware that in trying to grapple with the Holocaust he is examining something that stubbornly resists most intellectual and spiritual efforts. Many Jewish thinkers today simply stand in silence in the face of the Holocaust, even though they know that it is a central event in the history of modern Jewish life. Fackenheim's sensitivity to the difficulty and enormity of the endeavor to confront the Holocaust pervades his writings. At one time he said:

> There are hints or fragments which bespeak a meaning, but never sufficiently to provide an explanation. The theologian should not be concerned to explain history but, instead, to know how to live with it, and, in whatever way he can, to find God in it. That is why I said that I find a commanding voice of God in Auschwitz, but no redeeming voice. It is an instance of the self-revealing and self-concealing God.[34]

In looking at the Holocaust Fackenheim can do no more than to offer some "hints or fragments which bespeak a meaning." Yet, he finds himself obligated to speak instead of waiting for the fragments to fully blossom.

Rather than try to explain the Holocaust, Fackenheim has searched for an authentic response. He brings forward, at different times, three reasons for the necessity of a theological response. First, the event has already elicited an intense reaction from the Jewish community. Fackenheim understands that in the wake of the Holocaust "the long theological silence was necessary" but that now "the time of theological silence is irretrievably past."[35] The new period of speech and witnessing is marked by the fact that "among the people the flood-gates are broken."[36] Writing in 1968 Fackenheim said that two or three years earlier he had made the startling discovery that the Jewish community had already been responding to the Holocaust even though modern Jewish thinkers had by and large ignored it.[37] In light of this he felt obligated to both understand this response and give guidance to the community. Second, Fackenheim sees it as a sacred obligation to remember and witness to those who had been murdered. Finally, and most importantly, he writes that Jews "must refuse to disconnect God from the holocaust."[38] Fackenheim believes that the Jewish theologian must both respond to the Holocaust and somehow speak of its connection with God, or else God is taken out of the present; and, as we will see, to take God out of the present is to destroy the belief in the God of past or future.

## 98 What Does Revelation Mean for the Modern Jew?

The intensity and ubiquity of the treatment of the Holocaust in Fackenheim's later work evidences the fact that he regarded these reasons as overwhelming. Every book, essay, and lecture in which Fackenheim speaks of the Holocaust commences with his argument about the *uniqueness* of the event. For Fackenheim even the word "genocide" fails to capture the most important dimensions of this horrifying event. What distinguishes the Holocaust from all comparisons with other events of human history are the following features: First, six million Jews were killed not because of their faith or faithlessness, but because their great-grandparents continued to see themselves within the history of the covenant between God and Israel.[39] Second, the killing was an end in itself. Unlike the Inquisition, Jewish bodies were not destroyed in order to "save" Jewish souls. The killing of Jews was regarded as the Nazi's first priority, for at the end of the war this destruction took precedence over the war effort itself.[40]

Fackenheim attaches great significance to his characterization of the uniqueness of the Holocaust.[41] The fact that Jews were killed because of the faithfulness of their great-grandparents demonstrates, according to him, that the connection between the Holocaust and the history of Jewish belief is demanded even by the definition of the Jew which the Nazis themselves used. In recognizing that killing became a goal in itself, Fackenheim finds himself confronted with an example of "radical evil" that distinguishes the Holocaust from all other acts of genocide,[42] which evidence some kind of "rational" goal. These two features of Fackenheim's description of the Holocaust bring him to see it as a terrifying example of the Jewish "singled-out" condition. It is both tied to the history of Jewish belief and is shown by the radically evil nature of the event to be beyond comparison with other seemingly parallel events. Fackenheim thus affirms that even though the modern Jew might wish to try to divorce the Holocaust from the past and present of Jewish life before God, the event itself cancels out such attempts. It is a terrifying reminder that the Jew cannot escape his "singled-out" condition.

One procedure that Fackenheim has used to understand the

challenge that the Holocaust poses for Jewish faith utilizes the paradigms of the "epoch-making event" and the "root experience."[43] He asks whether the challenge of the Holocaust is similar to the challenges Jewish faith has faced in other times of great suffering. Can its effect upon the modern Jew be compared with the consequences of the destructions of the First and Second Temple, or the Expulsion from Spain, upon Jewish faith at those times? If the Holocaust fits into this framework, then one can speak of it in terms of an "epoch-making" event, that is, an event which brings faith into conflict with present experience. The epoch-making event endangers the continuity of Judaism, because it characterizes a tragedy which is so severe that it radically tests the ability of the Jews of a particular generation to appropriate the past events in which their faith is rooted. Fackenheim is saying that certain events, such as the destruction of the Second Temple, threatened to drive a wedge between past and present, because the Jews of that time found it difficult, if not impossible, to believe that there was One who directed history. The epoch-making event elicits such grave doubt about God's power over history that His revelations in the past, as at Sinai, can no longer be believed in or appropriated as meaningful by the Jews of that time. If, then, the Holocaust is similar to such tragedies of Jewish history, it has the power to completely undermine Judaism. Within the context of this view of the nature of the challenge of the Holocaust, Fackenheim writes:

> Yet today it seems that whereas other believers have reason to reject the God of history, a Jew has nothing less than an obligation. At Auschwitz, Jews were murdered, not because they had disobeyed the God of history, but rather because their great-grandparents had obeyed Him . . . Never, within or without Jewish history, have men anywhere had such a dreadful, such a horrifying, reason for turning their backs on the God of history.[44]

There are times when Fackenheim seems to take the category of "epoch-making event" as fully adequate to the nature of the Holocaust, despite its "uniqueness." The book that brought forward this category, *God's Presence in History,* suggests that the Holocaust will be treated as a threat of this type,[45] and in other places Fackenheim has compared the Holocaust to the destruction of the temples.[46] Nevertheless, Fackenheim is not fully satisfied that this category defines the place of the Holocaust in history or in Jewish consciousness.[47] In truth, he retains the category, but also utilizes another even more radical one. It is his description of the Holocaust as a "root experience," and his statements about the "commanding voice of God in Auschwitz" which represent his most consistent effort to come to terms with the Holocaust. This understanding has also thrown him into the center of intense and continual controversy.[48]

Fackenheim's discussion of the nature of the "epoch-making event" is interwoven with his analysis of the category of the "root experience." The manifestations of God's saving Presence at the Red Sea and God's commanding Presence at Sinai are root experiences, for they are the foundation of the Jew's belief in God's power and direction. In the case of such tragedies as the Expulsion from Spain, these root experiences come under severe questioning. The fact that Judaism continued beyond the Expulsion indicates that the root experiences of the Red Sea and Sinai eventually overcame the challenge of this particular epoch-making event. The distinguishing features of a root experience are these, according to Fackenheim:[49] 1) God's Presence is immediately given in the event "for the abiding astonishment of the witnesses."[50] 2) The event is both public and historical. 3) The event is accessible to later generations. A root experience is thus one which continually transforms Jewish consciousness and experience for it demonstrates that God acts in history. The later generations not only know of the past event, but—more importantly and wonderously—they are still able to participate, to reenact, to respond to God's Presence as mediated through the event. An astonishment abides not only for the duration of the lives of those who first experienced the miraculous event, but for the duration of the generations of the community. Through the category of "root experience," Fackenheim has restated the theological truth of the Biblical statement that all Israel, both past and future, stood at Sinai.

It is not difficult to agree with Fackenheim when he sees the Holocaust as a threat to the root experiences of Judaism. Perhaps the terror and horror of the Holocaust is so loud that the Voice of the Red Sea and of Sinai, the Voice of God's power and will to save, cannot be heard or believed. Yet, going beyond this view, Fackenheim seeks to portray the Holocaust *as* a root experience. He writes:

> For the religious Jew, who remains within the Midrashic framework, the Voice of Auschwitz manifests a divine Presence which, as it were, is shorn of all except commanding Power. *This* Power, however, is inescapable.[51]

Fackenheim's analysis of the Holocaust utilizes the same terms that he offers as distinctive characteristics of root experiences in Judaism. The Holocaust is obviously a public and historical event. This event is clearly "accessible" to those who live after it. In fact, the Holocaust is nothing less than inescapable, since the contemporary Jewish community finds itself forced to plumb the meaning of this event. Moreover, Fackenheim speaks in this connection of the "sacred duty" to remember it.[52] The interpretation of the Holocaust in terms of the first criterion, that God's Presence is seen in the event and that there is an abiding astonishment at His Presence, is obviously the shibboleth of the whole matter. However, we read that "the Voice of Auschwitz manifests a divine Presence,"[53] and that the juxtaposition of Auschwitz with later events in the history of the modern state of Israel causes the Jews to feel an "abiding astonishment."[54]

In one of his works Fackenheim writes that Elie Wiesel, the noted Jewish novelist, "compared the holocaust with Sinai in revelatory significance."[55] The comment about Wiesel is appropriate to Fackenheim's own work. Fackenheim describes the root experience of Sinai in terms of God's "commanding Presence." "A commanding Voice is heard" at Sinai and astonishment abides because "divinity is present in the commandment."[56] Similarly, in looking at the Holocaust

Fackenheim refers to the "commanding voice of God in Auschwitz"[57] and, again, "the Voice of Auschwitz manifests a divine Presence."[58] Tying Sinai and Auschwitz together Fackenheim writes:

> And the Jewish secularist, no less than the believer, is *absolutely singled out* by a Voice as truly *other* than man-made ideals—an imperative as truly *given*—as was the Voice of Sinai.[59]

Thus, the phrase "the commanding voice of God in Auschwitz" is not an accidental slip of the pen for Fackenheim. It is a continual affirmation, which reveals what he takes as his own deepest grasp of this event. Finally, just as the root experience of Sinai legislates to later generations through specific divine commandments, Fackenheim finds that the Voice of Auschwitz issues forth with a specific commandment, in fact, "the 614th commandment."[60]

There are many different formulations of this new "divine commandment"[61] that confronts the Jew who lives after the Holocaust. The general content of the commandment is fixed: the Jew is commanded to survive. In Fackenheim's work the commandment is often expressed through the negative formulation: "the authentic Jew of today is forbidden to hand Hitler yet another, posthumous victory."[62] The full statement and explanation of the commandment is as follows:

> Jews are forbidden to hand Hitler posthumous victories. They are commanded to survive as Jews, lest the Jewish people perish. They are commanded to remember the victims of Auschwitz lest their memory perish. They are forbidden to despair of man and his world, and to escape into either cynicism or otherworldliness, lest they cooperate in delivering the world over to the forces of Auschwitz. Finally, they are forbidden to despair of the God of Israel, lest Judaism perish. A secularist Jew cannot make himself believe by a mere act of will, nor can he be commanded to do so . . . And a religious Jew who has stayed with his God may be forced into new, possibly revolutionary relationships with Him. One possibility,

however, is wholly unthinkable. A Jew may not respond to Hitler's attempt to destroy Judaism by himself cooperating in its destruction. In ancient times, the unthinkable Jewish sin was idolatry. Today, it is to respond to Hitler by doing his work.[63]

At other places in his writings the commandment is also said to include the imperative of Jewish unity, of witnessing to the event, of hoping in the future.

Although Fackenheim's contention that there is a "commanding voice of God in Auschwitz" has not been altered since he first wrote of it, the enigmatic nature of the contention itself remains. Fackenheim's critics would agree that it would be tremendously significant and uplifting, to say the least, if one could detect a divine Voice issuing out of the horror of Auschwitz. Yet, it is certainly not clear to most Jewish thinkers, as it is to Fackenheim, that there truly is a Voice. In spite of the help that such a Voice would provide for modern Jews, one still feels compelled to ask whether there is indeed a "commanding voice of God in Auschwitz," that is, to inquire into the *evidence* that Fackenheim brings forward to support his view.

Of course, there is an intense debate among contemporary philosophers and theologians concerning the (factual) character of religious statements as well as the kind of evidence that "counts" for religious statements. Fackenheim does not present us with, as it were, hard evidence. However, by looking over Fackenheim's writings one can discover the major reasons that compel him to speak of the "commanding voice of God in Auschwitz."

The grounds for Fackenheim's belief that there is a divine Voice that issues forth from Auschwitz can be briefly summarized. Fackenheim notes that there are dimensions of contemporary Jewish life—Jewish witnessing to the story of the Holocaust, the stubborn refusal of Jews to abandon their Judaism, and the mysterious connection between Auschwitz and Jerusalem—that appear as almost unconscious, but nonetheless real responses to the commandment that Jews must survive. Fackenheim's belief in the divine Voice also has its basis in his conviction that the God of history is irretrievably lost if all that can be said about His relationship to the Holocaust is that there are times in history when God is silent. Rejecting the idea of a total divine eclipse, he discovers that there *is* a Voice to be heard.

According to Fackenheim, there are trends within contemporary Jewish life that must startle any observer. The fact of Jewish witnessing to the Holocaust is the first of these trends. Jews, both religious and non-religious, find that there is the "duty to remember and to tell the tale"[64] of the Holocaust. The duty is recognized as nonnegotiable, and even the non-religious Jew is forced to speak of it as "holy." While the religious Jew does not feel self-conscious in using this word to describe his feelings, "the secularist Jew is commanded to restore it."[65]

We have already alluded to the second trend, that is, the community's reaction to the Holocaust. When Fackenheim first began to look into the Holocaust, he was astonished to find that the Jewish community was already formulating, even if not fully consciously, a response to this event. Jews throughout the world were "stubbornly defying it [the Holocaust], committing themselves, if to nothing more, to the survival of themselves and their children as Jews."[66] Fackenheim believed that this dedication to Judaism could not be over-emphasized, since it arose out of the knowledge of what the recent past had brought and what could not be definitely ruled out of the future. He was left with no option but to see in this "a monumental act of faithfulness, as well as a monumental, albeit fragmentary, act of faith."[67]

The refusal of Jews to allow Judaism to die out through even natural causes, as it were, indicates to Fackenheim that the community is aware of God's action to prevent the unspeakable. This dimension of the contemporary Jewish commitment to Judaism is indicated in the way he phrases the "614th commandment:" "the authentic Jew of today is forbidden to hand Hitler yet another, posthumous victory."[68] The Jewish community recognizes that there is a moral imperative behind its endeavor to refuse to allow the seemingly insurmountable forces of assimilation to achieve Hitler's aim. While most Jews would not speak in terms of a divine commandment, Fackenheim sees in this behaviour an underlying acknowledgement that God

Himself is behind the struggle to prevent the possibility of Hitler's posthumous victory.

The relationship between "Auschwitz and Jerusalem" highlights, again, the Jewish refusal to abandon religious tradition. Fackenheim is not commenting at this point upon the complex historical relationship between the Holocaust and the founding of the state of Israel. He is looking into the relationship between the Holocaust, where annihilation was almost completed, and the 1967 Six-day War, where the threat was beaten back. He believes that the relationship between these two events was sensed by the whole Jewish community:

> When at Jerusalem in 1967 the threat of total annihilation gave way to sudden salvation it was because of Auschwitz, not in spite of it, that there was an abiding astonishment . . . Yet the very clash between Auschwitz and Jerusalem produced a moment of truth—a wonder at a singled out, millennial existence which, after Auschwitz, is still possible and actual.[69]

Fackenheim finds that the various aspects of these three areas of contemporary Jewish life force a particular interpretation upon the sensitive observer. These phenomena can only be understood as responses to a Voice which is heard throughout the community. While many would be hesitant to identify the Voice, Fackenheim declares that it is the commanding Voice of God coming out of the Holocaust.

Fackenheim's appreciation for the radical challenge that history presents for Jewish belief, an appreciation which we have identified as the core of his later theological development, is a central factor in his conviction that there is a "commanding voice of God in Auschwitz." His insight that Jewish theology must recognize both the significance of contemporary history and the possibility of God's entering into the present brought him to attest to this Voice. As we have seen, Fackenheim understood that "in faithfulness to Judaism we must refuse to disconnect God from the holocaust."[70] To completely separate God from the Holocaust is to discount God's Presence from the Jew's contemporary life. However, if God's direction in the present is denied, His revelations in the past as well as His promises for the future become highly dubious. Thus, the whole movement of Fackenheim's later theological thinking brought him to search for some connection between God and the Holocaust.

Fackenheim understands that God's actions in history are not always clear. There are times when the believer does not discern the meaning in what is going on, but has faith that there is meaning. It would seem that, rather than declare that there is a divine voice coming out of Auschwitz, Fackenheim could simply choose to write about God's silence or the eclipse of God. He does refer in many places to Martin Buber's image of the eclipse of God. Like so many others, Fackenheim was drawn to the view that, at least at this moment, God is silent either because He is not speaking or because man is not listening. Yet Fackenheim ultimately rejected this solution. In *God's Presence in History* he admits that Buber's image is able to sustain Jewish faith in its confrontation with secularism, but he adds that "this image fails to sustain us in our confrontation with the Nazi holocaust."[71] He continues, "If *all present* access to the God of history is *wholly* lost, the God of history is Himself lost."[72]

Much of Fackenheim's latest theological development is embodied in an affirmation that is at first self-evident and yet which reveals its full significance only after careful reflection: "the God of Israel cannot be God of either past or future unless He is still God of the present."[73] Fackenheim recognized that the believer's faith in God's direction of history, or in history's meaningfulness, cannot restrict itself to the past—the world of the Bible, or to the future—the Messianic Age. If the Jew denies the meaningfulness of the present, if he sees modern Jewish history as a complete dead end, then he has in fact lost his faith in the Lord of Israel. If one believes that God has lost His power or interest in the present, then grave questions arise about the meaning of the stories of His past actions in history and about His ability to fulfill the promises He has made for the future. Again, the theological options that allow one to disconnect God from the present, as in Deism, also bring an end to God's tie to Abraham as well as to His promises for Abraham's descendents. Of course, Fackenheim does not suggest that the Jew should be possessed by the illusion that he definitely "knows" God's plans at each point of time. The Jew should also not assume that whatever occurs in history by virtue of the fact that it happens is thereby given God's *hatima (imprimatur)*. The man of faith must move uneasily between the Scylla of ignoring the present and the Charybdis of accepting all.

Thus, Fackenheim finds that the modern Jew is obligated by his faith to connect God with the Holocaust; and he is forbidden, if he wishes to continue to hold to the faith of his fathers, to suggest that God is at this time totally silent. This insight plays an important role in Fackenheim's affirmation of the "commanding voice of God in Auschwitz." He is able to retain the faith of the fathers and to hold fast to the God of history, because he does hear a Voice coming out of the ashes of the Holocaust.

Fackenheim believes that the "Jewish return into history" signifies more than just the post-Holocaust age. The modern Jewish theologian is also compelled to reflect on the meaning of the founding of the State of Israel after two millennia of Jewish exile. While Fackenheim has acknowledged the magnitude of this "positive" challenge from the beginning of his new theological stance, he is not as eloquent in reflecting upon either the relationship between "Auschwitz and Jerusalem" or the unique challenge of Jerusalem as he is in treating the negative challenge of the Holocaust.

Fackenheim again finds that only fragmentary statements can be made about the bond between Auschwitz and Jerusalem. Yet, he writes, "it is necessary, not only to perceive a bond between the two events but also so to act as to make it unbreakable."[74] This bond eludes those who try to probe its meaning through historical or theological "explanations." What can be expressed is that Israel stands at the center of those efforts at Jewish survival that are also fed by the memory of Auschwitz. Israel's link with the Holocaust becomes most evident when challenges to its existence have the effect of intensifying both the remembering and the struggle for survival felt by the entire Jewish community.

The founding of the state of Israel confronts modern Jewish

thought with an event that eludes all purely secular categories. The Jewish theologian is forced to recognize the messianic dimension of Israel's very real new birth. Fackenheim's statement, "that in one sense (if not in many others) a long exile is ended,"[75] gives expression to one fragment of this dimension. And, once again, Fackenheim affirms that he is merely giving voice to a response already being lived out by the Jewish community. At one point he describes his astonishment at the fact that the Israeli Chief Rabbinate has composed a prayer for the synagogue service on *Shabbat* that refers to this messianic dimension of the state of Israel. The prayer beings, "Our Father in Heaven, the Rock of Israel and her Redeemer, bless Thou the state of Israel, the beginning of the dawn of our redemption . . ."[76]

In Fackenheim's book of 1982, *To Mend the World: Foundations of Future Jewish Thought,* his turn to history is affirmed in an even more stringent way. In this work he insists that in addition to Jewish faith, Christian faith and even philosophic thought cannot stand immune to the shattering historical event of our age, the Holocaust. There are two dimensions of this vulnerability to history that are new in this work, the radical critique that history offers for *all* thought, and the view that Jewish and Christian faith, as well as philosophic thought can continue today, *only* because of particular historical acts during the event of the Holocaust itself.

The themes that dominated the second and third period of Fackenheim's theological development are reaffirmed in this most recent work. Fackenheim discusses the importance of Rosenzweig and Buber for his own thought and for modern Jewish thought in general, the issue of revelation as the shibboleth of modern Jewish thought, the singled-out Jewish condition, the uniqueness of the Holocaust, and even the belief that there is a commanding Voice[77] that issues forth from that event. Of course, the Holocaust continues to be the central focus of

Fackenheim's work and it now stands not only as a challenge to Jewish thought and belief, but to philosophy and to Christianity. The Holocaust has resulted in a rupture that is worldwide in scope:

> But the Holocaust calls into question not this or that way of being human, but *all* ways. It ruptures civilizations, cultures, religions, not within this or that social or historical context, but within *all possible* contexts. Hence a *Tikkun* of the Holocaust (if a *Tikkun* there is) transcends its limited context in significance. It is Good News to the world. The thought we are in search of—philosophical, Christian, and Jewish itself—will therefore have one universality: that of a witness. Its *Tikkun* will be what in Jewish tradition *Tikkun* is always meant to be—*Tikkun Olam* [mending of the world].[78]

Fackenheim's appreciation of the necessity for an encounter with history, of demanding that one's thought be vulnerable to history, was deeply tied to his confrontation with the Holocaust. With this encounter over fifteen years old, the full radicalness of the threat of the Holocaust is now clear, according to Fackenheim. The maturing of his own thought has brought a fundamental change in the tone and the method of Fackenheim's writing. The tone or style of the book reflects the author's passionate commitment that condemns neutrality as evasion and dishonesty.[79] At times, the book becomes almost one long scream. The method has changed to a "historical-dialectical approach," where the views of thinkers of the first rank are confronted with "the events to which self-exposure is necessary."[80]

The treatment of the thought of Martin Heidegger is a paradigm for this change in tone and method. The existentialist "traditon" in philosophy has been of great interest to Fackenheim since his very first essays.[81] In particular, Heidegger as the highest example of this thrust in philosophy has been a "temptation" for Fackenheim for a long time.[82] His earlier critiques of Heidegger were aimed at his view that there is a single, universal, human condition to which philosophy must first attend. Fackenheim has insisted that not only are there a variety of such conditions, as there are a variety of types of human communities, but that the religious, philosophical, and moral riddles of contemporary Jewish existence have disclosed the inadequacy of any attempt to begin with such a single foundation.[83]

In the present treatment of Heidegger, Fackenheim finds inadequate not only the philosophy, but, more importantly, the actions of its author. The link between philosophy and action, which Heidegger himself insisted upon, becomes the decisive factor in Fackenheim's negative evaluation. He believes that Heidegger's own failure to speak out against Hitler, in fact his early support of Hitler that is expressed and justified in terms of his own philosophy, proves the *philosophical* bankruptcy of the thought itself.[84]

What is also new to these "foundations of future Jewish thought," the subtitle of the book, is that actions by particular individuals and groups are introduced as the "ontological" foundations for the *Tikkun* or mending that the tremendous "rupture" of the Holocaust necessitates. The acts of "resistance" by a particular philosopher, a single Christian, and a number of individuals and groups of Jews are said to both mend three dimensions of this rupture and to demand of all later people lives of resistance.

The use of the term *Tikkun* and the expression *Tikkun Olam* marks the first time that Fackenheim has incorporated the terminology of Jewish mysticism into the core of his work.[85] More importantly, the terms imply that there are partial acts of saving or redemption in history and that these acts have both a human and a divine dimension.[86] Thus, in speaking of *Tikkun,* even if only in fragmentary forms, Fackenheim is adding a very significant element to his understanding of contemporary history. Unlike his discussion of the commanding Voice, where there is a commanding but not saving Presence, his statements about particular acts of *Tikkun* and the results that still follow from them, introduces a divine saving Presence as well as the commanding Presence in connection to the Holocaust.

The first area of rupture and *Tikkun* that Fackenheim explores is that which occurred within philosophy. Philosophy was threatened in two ways by the Holocaust. First, taking a statement from Theodore Adorno, the ultimate horror of the Holocaust "paralyzed" not this or that philosophic thought but the whole "metaphysical capacity."[87] Philosophy was, and still often is, either immobilized, or it attempted to evade or escape the horror of the event. Second, philosophy's "noblest achievement," the Idea of humanity, was overturned by both the barbarity of the perpetrators and the living-death of the victims.[88] A fragmentary mending was brought to the philosophic tradition when a philosopher in the *name* of Philosophy resisted the Nazi endeavor. A philosophy professor, Kurt Huber, thus saved that tradition when he defended in court, in the name of the Kantian categorical imperative, some students who were accused of distributing anti-Nazi pamphlets in 1943.[89]

The rupture of the Christian tradition included "the Christian Good News that God saves in the Christ" and the Christian trust in the guidance of the Holy Spirit.[90] In fact, Fackenheim holds that one dimension of Christianity's precarious position in the modern world is the result of the silence of the churches, that is, their failure to witness against the Holocaust. In turn, the trust in both the Good News and the Spirit was partially mended, when Prior Bernhard Lichtenberg in 1938 publicly prayed in his church in Germany "on behalf of the Jews and the poor concentration camp prisoners."[91]

The Jewish tradition would also have been left doubly broken except for the actions of countless Jews, and some non-Jews, who resisted the irresistible. The rupture was between Jews and non-Jews and between post-Holocaust Jews and their Jewish tradition. The *Tikkun* to the relationship between Jews and non-Jews was first begun by those Christians who were not silent. The recovery of the tradition is possible because of the various types of resistance that Jews offered in the face of the paramount Nazi goal of destroying not only Jewish lives, but the humanity of their Jewish victims.[92]

The mending of philosophy, Christianity, and Judaism was only begun at the time of the Holocaust. According to Fackenheim, these first steps made all later acts of mending both possible and obligatory. He concludes his treatment of the *Tikkun* in terms of the Jewish tradition with the statement that *"the*

*Tikkun which for the post-Holocaust Jew is a moral necessity is a possibility because during the Holocaust itself a Jewish Tikkun was already actual.'*[93]

Finally, Fackenheim sees the modern state of Israel as the highest example of the powerful mending, the *Tikkun,* that post-Holocaust Jews find in their midst today.[94] Fackenheim's latest work thus understands the existence of the state of Israel as a human and divine activity that stands at the center of all authentically Jewish thought and work in our time.[95]

The preceding treatment of Fackenheim's understanding of the Holocaust and the founding of the State of Israel commenced with the statement that the radical turn in Fackenheim's theology was neither fortuitous nor the outcome of some idiosyncratic moods. Fackenheim's "vulnerability" to history rests upon the twin foundations of his dissatisfaction with his earlier way of proceeding and his recognition of the threat that the Holocaust poses for Jewish belief. However, despite these foundations, the crucial questions still remain: Is God speaking? Do we live in the midst of a divine and human *Tikkun*?

We see that Fackenheim is desperately trying to listen for some hint of a sound from God. Yet, it is legitimate to ask whether he tries too hard and thus transforms his endeavor to hear into a hearing. Does Fackenheim just misread some dimensions of contemporary Jewish life—the witnessing to the Holocaust, the affirmation of Jewish survival, the connection between "Auschwitz and Jerusalem"—either by noting trends that are not there or by interpreting a false cause for some very real phenomena? Does he turn a forceful religious argument—the inadequacy of a divine "eclipse" at this moment—that stresses the need for God's voice, into a way of fabricating God's voice? These questions can best be condensed into one further question: Is all this talk about the "commanding voice of God in Auschwitz" nothing more than the newest illustration that Freud was correct when he applied the

Emil Fackenheim 113

term "wish-fulfillment" to the phenomenon of religious belief?

Additionally, the latest expression of this vulnerability to history has only increased our questions. While every act of resistance during the Holocaust necessarily elicits a radical surprise and a feeling of deep indebtedness from all of those who follow later, can we legitimately give these acts "ontological" status? Has Fackenheim with this *Tikkun* now passed even those limits that he set for himself, when he earlier affirmed that there could not be a divine saving Presence in connection with the Holocaust even if there could be a commanding one?[96]

The answer to these questions are not easily forthcoming. However, before too hastily dismissing Fackenheim's position, we must recognize the fundamental challenges that Fackenheim, in turn, might pose: The hearing of the "commanding voice of God in Auschwitz" is founded on a leap and a wanting to hear, but can there ever be any hearing unless there is a desperate need to hear? Could those who did not believe that they needed direction hear when God spoke through the clouds and thunder at Sinai? Is there any other way than through a leap and a commitment to allow oneself the possibility of being radically surprised?

A conclusive answer to the above sets of queries would require us to abandon the present task of philosophical analysis and attempt to give voice to our own hearing or not hearing. While this is clearly beyond the scope of this presentation, the questions still have meaning in pointing to both the shadows and the areas of light in Fackenheim's presentation.

Fackenheim has remained true to his belief that it is blasphemous to explain the Holocaust, but that the Jewish thinker is forced to confront it, and the founding of Israel, with all the strength at his command. Fackenheim's conviction that the modern Jewish theologian must struggle intensely and seriously with these two events is clearly embodied in the main thrust of his later theological development.

As a Jew and as one who believes that he can provide some direction to the modern Jewish community, Fackenheim recognizes that he must struggle with the meaning of these two events. He is conscious of the tension between important latent Jewish responses to these events and the great hesitancy and fear that sensitive Jews feel when approaching these subjects. Yet he feels compelled to speak, knowing that waiting itself might only lessen the recuperative powers, the *Tikkun*(?), that the Jewish community holds within.

## Chapter V
# Conclusion: Wrestling with the Category of Revelation

In the preceding treatments of the individual religious transformations of Franz Rosenzweig, Martin Buber, and Emil Fackenheim we have defined and diagrammed some of the central dimensions of modern religious man's wrestling with the category of revelation. Rosenzweig's movement from philosophy to religion represents his rejection of the dogma of human self-sufficiency for an understanding that only God's revelation brings orientation, or a fullness to life in this world. In Buber's life there is the movement from the conviction that the divine is a dimension of the human to a belief that dialogue with the eternal Thou is the apex as well as the force behind relationship to others. Fackenheim found that his earlier understanding of the nature of revelation had too tightly circumscribed God's relationship to man. His theological development was based on the insight that God's Presence is still active on the historical stage.

The problems and solutions of Rosenzweig, Buber, and Fackenheim are more than individual, idiosyncratic explorations; but are paradigmatic of the problems that beset modern religious man. In *The Star of Redemption* Rosenzweig makes the interesting point that since the Enlightenment, theology has been very uneasy with miracles. He comments that during the Middle Ages miracles were central to the arguments between the three competing religious communities, but that they are now regarded with embarrassment and discarded as unwanted ballast by all.[1] Rosenzweig's insight can be extended to include the whole category of revelation, in which the issue of miracles finds a small place. Since the nineteenth century, religious thinkers, following the "emergence of philosophy of religion,"[2] have sought a human source for religion and either disowned revelation or denuded it of any meaning.

A number of paths have been taken by religious thinkers in the modern age in order to be in harmony with the thinking of the "enlightened." These paths permitted the religious person to both retain some kind of contact with religion and to be perceived as intellectually respectable, that is, modern. The only thing that this respectable religiosity cost was an appreciation of the reality of revelation. From this angle, it can be seen that Rosenzweig, Buber, and Fackenheim confront some of the fundamental *temptations* that haunt modern religious man's stance toward revelation. Rosenzweig's movement from philosophy symbolized his rejection of philosophy's right to either claim the truth of revelation as its own or to set aside revelation in the name of human authenticity. For Buber romanticism's reduction of God to a dimension of human feeling or creativity was a strong and lasting temptation. Fackenheim's later theological development results from his escape from the temptation to relegate God's action in history to the distant past, if not to *illo tempore*.

What is the nature of the temptation that was symbolized by the term "Philosophy" in Rosenzweig's purview? Philosophy's premise is that human autonomy leads to the only true authenticity. The older variety of this discipline, which ran from Iona to Jena, culminated in Hegel's systematics. Hegel annihilated the claims that revelation makes on man by swallowing up revelation into the history of man's consciousness of himself or Spirit. Rosenzweig believed that this variety died with Hegel and he never did feel the force of its ratiocinative enchantment.

Rosenzweig did at first succumb to the newer species of philosophy, the origins of which he traced to Kierkegaard, Schopenhauer, and Nietzsche. Rosenzweig described this as "point-of-view" philosophy. It held that the real basis of philosophy was not abstract reason, but the philosopher himself, as a man of flesh and blood. This existentialist stream continued to sing the praises of human autonomy and to dismiss the claims of revelation. Revelation was in this case condemned for alienating man from himself. The new philosophy regarded revelation as an obstacle to human authenticity, because belief in revelation directed man to truths that had their origin outside the individual and his lonely struggle to discover truth for himself. For both the old and new philosopher, thus, truth was the outcome of a heroic struggle. Rosenzweig's image of the tragic hero of Greek times fully agrees with this picture. The tragedy, and therefore the charm, of the philosopher's attitude toward the world is heightened by the newer breed who deny their forerunner's insistence that the truth they discovered was both objective and eternal. Nietzsche and those who followed him gave up the claims to objective and eternal truth and were satisfied to grasp what was true for them even if their answers carried no force beyond their own lives.

This heroic portrait of the isolated man who stakes all on his own powers is a temptation for modern religious men. Certainly many have admired the struggle of men such as Nietzsche and Camus to find the truth; and they have looked down upon religious believers who, in their eyes, use God as a crutch to ease the way. It seems that in the encounter with Rosenstock, Rosenzweig found that authentic religious men do not cease to struggle and do not choose the easy way. Rosenzweig discovered that it is not the philosopher, but the religious man who is the true hero. In living with God man lives deeply in the world and authenticates the truth as it is given to him. Rosenzweig's movement from philosophy to religion was thus the outcome of his understanding that the path to authenticity lay not through the efforts of the autonomous, isolated man, but through the meetings of the religious man with others in the world. Thus, for Rosenzweig, the living reality of the relationship to God allows man to escape the temptation that philosophy offers.

Martin Buber fully faced the temptation that the neo-romantic interest in mysticism posed, and still poses, for modern religious men. For a young man who intensely felt the divisions within the self and the lack of harmony between the self and the world, mysticism offered an immediate answer. Mysticism said that the Self held all within itself. The relationship to God was no longer something that implied a turning without and a responsibility to the world. God was experienced—but not encountered—in either the flush of inner feeling or the heights of gratifying creativity. In essence both the isolated mystic reveling in his own feelings and the creative artist reveling in his products substitute aestheticism for the life with others—the duty of loving the neighbour—which religion demands. It took two decades for Buber to pull himself away from these temptations. His dawning awareness that real life with others should not be shunned offered the first insight into the illusions of aestheticism. Buber began to realize that the self is only real in relation to a distinct but caring other. He finally found that authenticity is a quality of that life which is lived in dialogue with others and that this dialogue always points beyond itself to the dialogue with God.

Emil Fackenheim was also caught up in a temptation, the temptation that crystallizes in what has been termed religious existentialism. Religious existentialism, best represented by Soren Kierkegaard, often offers an attenuated concept of revelation for the fullness of the relationship between man and God. This stream of thought does not demand rejection of God. It fervently proclaims that the authentic life is lived in relationship to God, but its portrait of the dimensions of this relationship are what tempts many modern religious people. Existentialism, as Fackenheim early embraced it, ignored the individual's tie to his community and its history and accentuated the splendid isolation of the individual before the infinite God. The turning point in Fackenheim's theological development occurred when he discovered that religious people could not be abstracted out of the history of their religious community. Fackenheim affirmed that, in particular, the Jew stands not alone before the wholly Other, but within the history of that covenant that God established with the Jewish people. He also recognized that since the Jew must always be understood within convenantal history, His relationship to God cannot ignore the present history of that

Wrestling with the Category of Revelation 119

community. Fackenheim rejected the temptation to make history the affair solely of man with man and man with nature. He noted that many modern religious people refused to speak of the possibility of radical surprise, that is, of the possibility of God's action in history. In consequence of this they surrendered that dimension of revelation that guarded against the relationship to God becoming solely a matter of what the individual "does with his own solitariness."[3] The event of the Holocaust awakened Fackenheim to the danger of divesting the category of revelation of its meaning. In rejecting the temptation of religious existentialism, he was able to look again for God's Presence in history.

In all three cases, these temptations to the religious life focus on the issue of isolation versus the life with others. Rosenzweig's rejection of philosophy is his movement toward a way of life in which "God, man, and the world reveal themselves only in their relations to one another, that is, in creation, revelation, and redemption . . ."[4] Buber's repudiation of mysticism evidenced his disillusionment with its solitariness and its disparagement of everyday life. His philosophy of dialogue, in contrast, glorified the day-to-day living with other men and with God. Finally, Fackenheim's critique of much of modern theology, as we have just seen, opposed its withdrawal of the religious life from history and community.

Yet, despite the struggles of Rosenzweig, Buber, and Fackenheim to overcome the temptations or threats to the religious life that have just been examined, their solutions are not unambiguous. Although the theme of the movement from philosophy to religion is a key to the personal and intellectual development of Franz Rosenzweig, he also proposed that the authentic person is both religious man *and* philosopher. He wrote in the *Star* that

> God's truth conceals itself from those who reach for it with one hand only . . . It is the same man, disbelieving child of the world and believing child of God in one, who comes with dual plea and must stand with dual thanks before Him who gives of his wisdom to flesh and blood even as to those who fear him.[5]

Rosenzweig thus held that the only way to authenticity was to live as both religious man and philosopher. To live fully in the modern world demands a combination of these two ways of life and thought. On the one hand, it is illegitimate to turn away from modernity with its independence and its skepticism and blindly assert that it is really only God's plan that matters. On the other hand, to celebrate man's new-found enlightenment and his residence in the secular world without worrying also about the individual's isolation is an illusory path. The most difficult stance of all, that of being both questioning religious man and trusting philosopher, is the only real option open to modern men.

Although Buber eventually renounced the mysticism that early fascinated him, it had by that time permeated to the marrow of his bones. Traces of mysticism's earlier hold over him remain. As we have seen, the most important statement of the philosophy of dialogue, *I and Thou,* contains many disconcerting elements of Buber's earlier thought. In these elements one sees Buber's desire for a unification with the world of nature and also an indistinct drawing of the divine-human relationship in which the one side seems to merge with the other. Buber's intense feelings of alienation never left him. He saw the lack of unity and harmony as a permanent part of the human condition as well as a particularly depressing undercurrent of modern life. After fervent searchings for clarity and truth Buber did maintain that the most authentic way of life was the life of dialogue with other men and with God. Yet, he also continued to give poetic expression to the goal of a deeper harmony with nature and with God than the philosophy of dialogue permitted.

The nature of the ambiguity of Fackenheim's solution sets it apart from the synthesizing solution of Rosenzweig and the poetic interplay of Buber's resolution. Fackenheim's renunciation of his earlier theological positions was final, although he did continue to highlight the existentialist's concern with tension, paradox, and the data of men's lives in the world. One can see the strength and justice of Fackenheim's critique of his earlier positions and those who represent that religious point of view; but that does not dispel the questions that his new position

## Wrestling with the Category of Revelation 121

immediately brings forth. We have enumerated those questions at the end of the last chapter: Has he tried too hard to find God's Presence in the present so that the endeavor to hear in time came to be a hearing? Has he turned arguments that stress the need for God's Voice into a way of fabricating that Voice? Is a divine and human *Tikkun* really to be found within that utter blackness known as the Holocaust?

Still, it is not difficult to account for these ambiguities. It might be best to speak again of temptations and the struggles to overcome them. The ambiguities reflect the fact that the temptations were real and powerful and that their power could never be fully escaped. Rosenzweig found that for modern man there is no "either/or" between philosophy and religion. To be thrust into the world in the deepest way one must be a "disbelieving child of the world and believing child of God in one." For Buber, modern man's need for unity and harmony could not adequately be met by any single philosophy, even the dynamics of the philosophy of I and Thou. Fackenheim was able to see the limits of one of the prevailing portraits of revelation, but his "fragmentary answer" is almost as unsatisfactory as what preceded it. In all, the ambiguities reflect the difficulty of the problems with which these men wrestled. In light of the nature of modern religious life, one wonders whether any less troublesome solutions could faithfully mirror the world of these men and ourselves.

While it has not been suggested that there is any kind of hierarchy or order in the three preceding treatments, one way of looking at the whole instead of just the individual parts is to recognize that Fackenheim's statement is an important step beyond his predecessors. This has been hinted at previously and it is important to unravel that hint at this time. Fackenheim's "vulnerability" to history points to a deficiency in the understandings of revelation of Rosenzweig and Buber and he seeks to overcome this deficiency.

Fackenheim's earliest theological standpoint owed much to the thought of Rosenzweig and Buber. Fackenheim characterizes their influence on him in terms of their portrayal of man's life in the Presence of Him who still addresses and hears. In this connection Fackenheim has written that "Buber and Rosenzweig gave a radical Jewish response to the challenge of the modern world . . . for they sought nothing less than a modern presence of the ancient God."[6] We have already seen that Rosenzweig's *Star* has as its center the divine-human encounter which gives man a new orientation in the world. Similarly, Buber's *I and Thou* stands as the most eloquent expression written in this century of the life of dialogue between God and man. Both thinkers, in addition, sought to dispel the façade of self-satisfaction that modern man exhibits when he surveys himself and the world. They spoke of the fragmentariness of much of modern life and of the need to turn to the One who continually addresses man. Certainly Fackenheim's early polemic against liberalism and secularism drew heavily upon this critique as well as upon Rosenzweig's and Buber's understandings of the significance of revelation for modern man.

However, it is important to recognize that the major changes in Fackenheim's theological outlook represents a critique of the thought of Rosenzweig and Buber. While both Jewish philosophers gave witness to the God who turns to man, the historical and communal dimensions of God's revelation were either minimized or ignored.

There are three aspects of revelation that Rosenzweig details in his writings. First, God addresses the individual in the midst of his daily life in the world. The individual comes away from this dialogue with a sense of mission, because he understands that he shares in the divine plan. Second, Rosenzweig described the believer's access to God's Presence through the liturgy of the community.[7] Third, Rosenzweig spoke of God's revelations in the past, within history, that founded the two religious communities of Judaism and Christianity. Thus, for Rosenzweig, while the Voice of God is still alive in the present, He has ceased to speak into history. Fackenheim once summarized Rosenzweig's position in the *Star* by saying that Jewish history is circumscribed by two poles. One marks the shofar that was blown at Sinai and the other is represented by the sound of the shofar that will signify the eschatological end of time. Fackenheim concluded that for Rosenzweig "nothing decisive has happened or can happen between these two poles."[8]

Buber's view of revelation is even more individual-oriented and ahistorical. His alienation from communal institutions, liturgy, and Law led him to drop the second of Rosenzweig's characterizations of revelation, that is, that found within the community's "sacred year." In addition, Buber does not believe that any revelations in the past, including Sinai, stand as supremely important moments in the divine-human dialogue. Sinai is a good model of the nature of the encounter between God and man, but it is not essentially different from the Word of God that is available to people today. Consequently, the scope of the dialogue between God and man is confined by Buber to those moments of encounter that the individual discovers in the midst of his living in the world.

Fackenheim recognized that the biblical God is lost not only by denying the possibility of His revelation to the individual in the present, but also by ignoring the possibility of His present action in history. Fackenheim's words, once again, state this point in all of its power: "the God of Israel cannot be God of either past or future unless He is still God of the present." This new "vulnerability" to history is thus a significant addition to the inheritance that modern religious thought has received from the work of Rosenzweig and Buber. Rosenzweig endeavored to make the significance of revelation come alive for modern man. Buber sought to open a window to the exchange of "I" and "Thou" between man and God. Fackenheim endeavored to sensitize the modern religious person to the possibilities of God's actions in the present.

We will conclude this exploration of the meaning of revelation in the thought of Rosenzweig, Buber, and Fackenheim by examining the relationship between their dynamic solutions and that funadamental and uniquely Jewish embodiment as well as response to revelation, Halacha. Although we have briefly touched upon this subject in passing up to this point, it is essential that their different attitudes toward Halacha be raised, once again, in a more systematic way, in order to complete our portrait of their work as *Jewish* philosophers. We will see that these views of Halacha powerfully reflect their wrestling with the meaning of revelation. The quest to testify to the presence of God's voice in the life of the Jewish community was an important factor in their very independent, unorthodox views of the nature and significance of Jewish law.

Although Rosenzweig discusses the significance of Halacha in the *Star,* a few of his letters and smaller essays present his most systematic views. Rosenzweig saw the Law as playing a central role in the life of the Jewish community and the individual. Halacha both embodied God's commands to Israel and provided the opportunity for Jews to live out their response to these commands:

> [the] Law as a whole, is the prerequisite for being chosen, the law whereby divine election is turned into human electing, and the passive state of a people being chosen and set apart is changed into the activity on the people's side of doing the deed which sets it apart.[9]

Rosenzweig believed that a clear boundary could not be drawn between that aspect of the Law that was from God and that which was man's interpretation of the divine revelation. While not denying the importance of biblical criticism, he held that in the act of living out Halacha, the individual continually is made aware that God still speaks to the Jew through this instrument.[10] In exploring the disagreement between Buber and Rosenzweig concerning the possibility of hearing God's voice in acting out the Halacha, we will diagram both of their most important insights concerning this subject.

"The Builders," one of Rosenzweig's most important and well known essays, was first written as a letter in response to one of Buber's lectures on Judaism, "Herut: On Youth and Religion." In the letter, Rosenzweig indicates his strong disagreement with Buber's dogmatic insistence that the whole area of Jewish law be treated as unalterably dead and irrelevant to the present and future of the Jew. Rosenzweig emphasized that he understood and translated the term "Law" as commandment, commandment from God. "Law [*Gesetz*] must again become commandment [*Gebot*] which seeks to be transformed into deed at the very moment it is heard."[11] The Jew appropriates the commandments into his life as he finds himself directly addressed by God in or through them. In fact, Rosenzweig believed that since the Law continues as the instrument for hearing and responding to God's present commandments, it was inauthentic for the Jew to just go on "keeping" particular laws, if he did not do it for the sake of that divine voice.[12]

The final consequence of Rosenzweig's view of the Law as living commandment is that he saw the process of appropriating the Law into one's life as, in fact, a process. He rejects the paradigm that the Jew must either accept or reject the Law as one unalterable block of 613 commandments. He discusses the possibility not only that Jews will legitimately decide to leave unappropriated some aspects of the Law which are not alive for them, but that particular actions and customs that Jews believe bring them into contact with the divine voice should be incorporated into the domain of the Law.[13]

Buber's attitude toward the Law was in fundamental disagreement with that of Rosenzweig, and as with the latter, this attitude truly reflected a general philosophy of revelation. Before examining Buber's replies to Rosenzweig's criticisms, we will explore his position as indicated in *I and Thou* and some of the earlier writings. The understanding in *I and Thou* of the nature of revelation has already been discussed in the chapter on Buber. He held that revelation was an "eternal," "primal phenomenon," that is, that it is eternally the same and no event of revelation is different from others, except as it is interpreted by the one who receives and responds to it. Further, although Buber distinguishes three characteristics of this phenomenon, he finds that there is no clear content in it. In a statement that clearly is meant to refer to the subject of Jewish law, he writes:

> But even as the meaning itself [from revelation] cannot be transferred or expressed as a universally valid and generally ac-

> ceptable piece of knowledge, putting it to the proof in action cannot be handed on as a valid ought; it is not prescribed, not inscribed on a table that could be put up over everybody's head. The meaning we receive can be put to the proof in action only by each person in the uniqueness of his being and in the uniqueness of his life. No prescription can lead us to the encounter, and none leads from it.[14]

This statement that revelation can never be objectified into universal law is completely consistent with his critique of the views and institutions of Rabbinic Judaism in earlier writings. Buber's thoroughly discussed religious anarchism and antinomianism[15] was first expressed in a number of very one-sided contrasts. He contrasted those periods of dynamic religious experience and life (religiosity) with those periods of the deadening institutionalization of religion (religion) and he compared the lively subterranean Judaism of mystics and heretics with the fosselized Judaism of the later Rabbis.

In the exchange of letters with Rosenzweig concerning the Law, Buber again unequivocally expressed his understanding that Jewish law is *not* a legitimate instrument for living out the dialogue or relationship with God. He wrote,

> I do not believe that *revelation* is ever a formulation of law. It is only through man in his self-contradiction that revelation becomes legislation.[16]

> I told you that for me, though man is a law-receiver, God is not a law-giver, and therefore the Law has no universal validity for me . . .[17]

Finally, while Fackenheim's attitude toward the law has much in common with Rosenzweig and not much with Buber, there is an ambiguity in his work once he began to turn to the event of the Holocaust. In the essay of his first period, "An Outline of a Modern Jewish Theology," he held that once the Jew stands within the circle of Jewish faith, there is the possibility that any particular laws can be experienced as divine commands. Fackenheim, consistent with his stance within the Reform

Jewish community, did not see the Law as a single block or as a static guarantee of the relationship between God and the individual Jew. Still, he regarded it as more than just the product of human interpretation:

> The God-Israel-relation demands of the Jew, in addition to the moral response, a response expressing his Jewishness in all its particularity. This response is Halachah . . . Halachah is Jewish custom and ceremony mediated through the leap into Jewish faith; and it thereby becomes the divine law to Israel . . . And thus each of them [the commandments] has the potency of becoming Halachah, commanded and fulfilled: if fulfilled, not as self-expression but as response on the part of Israel to a divine challenge to Israel; as the gift of the Jewish self to God.[18]

In other essays of the second and of the latest period of his thought Fackenheim continues to hold this attitude toward the Law and often speaks of the "divine commanding Presence" that the Jew experiences in responding to and acting out the commandments. However, once Fackenheim begins to explore the challenge that the Holocaust poses for Jewish faith, he sees that the Holocaust may have the power to stand between the commandments and the Jew's experience of God's commanding Presence. In *God's Presence in History*, the Holocaust, as the most radical example of an "epoch-making event," clearly posseses the power of destroying that access to the divine Presence that has always linked together the generations of Jews into the covenant with God. It is not just the belief in the God of history who is threatened by the challenge of the murder of six million Jews.

As we know, Fackenheim reclaims both the God of history and his Presence in the commandments by discovering that God's commanding Presence is connected with the Holocaust. At one time he formulated this Presence in terms of the "614th commandment." Similarly, in *To Mend the World,* he holds that Torah is again a viable instrument for the Jew's experience of the divine Presence, because of the partial acts of *Tikkun* that were embodied in the resistance of the Jews during the time of the Holocaust. However, it must be added that once Fackenheim began to respond to the threat that the Holocaust poses for Jewish faith, his earlier portrait of God's Presence in the Halacha became overshadowed by the problem of His appearance or absence in connection with that event.

For Rosenzweig and Fackenheim, the insistence on God's revelation in the *present* led them to a not unequivocal attitude toward Halacha. Both of these Jewish philosophers rejected the notion of a single block of commandments. Rosenzweig's experience of the actuality of God's Presence in some of the commandments led him to insist that the Jew experience that Presence or desist, for a while, from fulfilling particular commandments. Fackenheim's belief that God could not be absent from the event of the Holocaust, led him to affirm that *only* if the community could experience a fragment of His Presence in connection with the Holocaust, was His Presence in Halacha a possibility. Finally, for Buber, revelation between God and man is such a unique dialogue that he maintained that no universal Law could arise from this meeting.

Thus, as with their efforts to reject the modern challenges or temptations to man's belief in God's revelation, so with their understandings of Halacha, one sees deep struggles with no unequivocal conclusions. Yet, as all three of these modern Jewish philosophers affirm, their struggles are not meant to provide conclusive solutions, but to point the way for other people. Together these Jewish philosophers have helped modern religious people to reclaim some dimensions of that Voice so confidently heard by Israel's fathers.

# NOTES

## Chapter I: Introduction

1. Abraham J. Heschel, *Who Is Man?* (Stanford, California: Stanford University Press, 1965), p. 1.
2. *Franz Rosenzweig: His Life and Thought,* ed. Nahum N. Glatzer (New York: Schocken Books, 1961), p. 97. Hereafter cited as *Franz Rosenzweig.*
3. Rosenzweig speaks of the individual's first and last names in order to emphasize the particularity and uniqueness of each person. See, for example, Franz Rosenzweig, *The Star of Redemption,* trans. from the Second Edition of 1930 by William W. Hallo (Boston: Beacon Press, 1972), p. 7. Hereafter cited as *Star.*
4. Emil L. Fackenheim, *God's Presence in History: Jewish Affirmations and Philosophical Reflections* (New York: Harper & Row, Harper Torchbooks, 1970), p. 31. Hereafter cited as *God's Presence.*
5. Emil L. Fackenheim, "The Commandment to Hope: A Response to Contemporary Jewish Experience," in *The Future of Hope,* ed. Walter H. Capps (Philadelphia: Fortress Press, 1970), p. 101. Hereafter cited as "Hope."
6. *Ibid.,* p. 100.
7. Nietzsche's statement is cited in Rosenzweig, *Star,* p. 18.
8. Sigmund Freud, *The Future of an Illusion,* trans. W.D. Robson-Scott and ed. James Strachey (Garden City, New York: Doubleday & Company, Anchor Books, 1964), pp. 23-24.
9. For a more detailed discussion of these characteristics of modern Jewish philosophy see Michael Oppenheim, "Some Underlying Issues of Modern Jewish Philosophy," in Howard Joseph, Jack Lightstone, and Michael Oppenheim, eds., *Truth and Compassion: Essays on Judaism and Religion in Memory of Rabbi Dr. Solomon Frank* (Waterloo, Ontario: Canadian Corporation for Studies in Religion, 1983), pp. 91-109.
10. Among the most important Jewish philosophers who challenged the rationalism of classical liberal Judaism are Eugene

Borowitz, Abraham Heschel, Will Herberg, Milton Steinberg, and Jacob Petuchowski. There are developments in the thought of Arthur A. Cohen that parallel some of Fackenheim's intellectual changes. See Cohen's latest book, *The Tremendum: A Theological Interpretation of the Holocaust* (New York: Crossroad, 1981).

## Chapter 2: Franz Rosenzweig

1. Franz Rosenzweig, *Briefe,* ed. Edith Rosenzweig and Ernst Simon (Berlin: Schocken Verlag, 1935), p. 469.
2. *Franz Rosenzweig,* p. 97.
3. Much of the information used here and in the following pages about the events in Rosenzweig's life is dependent on Nahum Glatzer's treatment in *Franz Rosenzweig.*
4. *Franz Rosenzweig,* pp. 18-20.
5. Glatzer's account of these discussions is in *Franz Rosenzweig,* pp. xiii-xvi, 23-25. The intellectual background for these discussions, including some of Rosenzweig's unpublished diary material, is given in Paul R. Mendes-Flohr and Jehuda Reinharz, "From Relativism to Religious Faith: The Testimony of Franz Rosenzweig's Unpublished Diaries," *Year Book XXII,* Publications of the Leo Baeck Institute (London: Secker & Warburg, 1977), pp. 161-174.
6. Rosenstock's letter is included in Rosenzweig, *Briefe,* p. 639, quoted in *Judaism Despite Christianity: The "Letters on Christianity and Judaism" between Eugen Rosenstock-Huessy and Franz Rosenzweig,* ed. Eugen Rosenstock-Huessy (New York: Schocken Books, Schocken Paperback, 1971), p. 32. Other letters in the correspondence of that year between Rosenzweig and Rosenstock are included in *Briefe,* pp. 641-720.
7. Rosenzweig, *Briefe,* p. 71, quoted and trans. by Alexander Altmann, "Franz Rosenzweig and Eugen Rosenstock-Huessy: An Introduction to Their 'Letters on Judaism & Christianity,'" in *Judaism Despite Christianity,* pp. 32-33.
8. Altmann discusses this in "Franz Rosenzweig and Eugen Rosenstock-Huessy," p. 30. Paul Mendes-Flohr and Jehuda Reinharz discuss the nature of Rosenzweig's relativism in "From Relativism to Religious Faith."
9. Rosenzweig, *Briefe,* quoted in *Judaism Despite Christianity,* p. 98.
10. *Franz Rosenzweig,* pp. 24-25.
11. *Franz Rosenzweig,* pp. 341-344.
12. A description of this experience is given by Rivka Horwitz, "Judaism Despite Christianity," *Judaism* 95 (Summer 1975): 316-318.
13. The insight that Rosenzweig's experience during the Day of Atonement is reflected in his *The Star of Redemption* is sug-

gested by Nahum Glatzer in the "Foreword" to the *Star*, xii.
14. Rosenzweig, *Star*, p. 323.
15. *Ibid.*, p. 324.
16. *Ibid.*, pp. 327-328.
17. *Franz Rosenzweig*, pp. 27-28.
18. *Franz Rosenzweig*, xx.
19. *Ibid.*, p. 28.
20. Rosenzweig's essay "Atheistische Theologie" is included in Franz Rosenzweig, *Kleinere Schriften* (Berlin: Schocken Verlag, 1937).
21. Rosenzweig, *Briefe*, quoted in *Judaism Despite Christianity*, p. 117.
22. Rosenstock's letter is in Rosenzweig, *Briefe*, quoted in *Judaism Despite Christianity*, pp. 119-120.
23. See " 'Urzelle' Des Stern Der Erlösung," a letter to Rudolf Ehrenberg in Rosenzweig, *Kleinere Schriften*, pp. 357-372.
24. *Franz Rosenzweig*, p. 87.
25. Rosenzweig's essay "Das Neue Denken," is included in Rosenzweig, *Kleinere Schriften*, p. 397.
26. *Franz Rosenzweig*, pp. 95-97.
27. Franz Rosenzweig, *Jehuda Halevi* (Berlin: L. Schneider, 1927).
28. Franz Rosenzweig, *Understanding the Sick and the Healthy*, trans. and ed. N.N. Glatzer (New York: The Noonday Press, 1953).
29. An analysis of Rosenzweig's concept of common sense is given in Nathan Rotenstreich, "Common Sense and Theological Experience," *Journal of the History of Philosophy*, Vol. 4 (1967): 353-360.
30. Rosenzweig, "Das Neue Denken," pp. 373-398.
31. A treatment of Hegel is given in the first section of the *Star*, pp. 3-22.
32. Rosenzweig, *Star*, p. 11.
33. *Ibid.*, p. 10.
34. Franz Rosenzweig, *Der Stern der Erlösung*, in *Franz Rosenzweig: Der Mensch Und Sein Werk, Gesammelte Schriften II*, (Haag: Martinus Nijhoff, 1976), p. 15. Hereafter cited as *Stern*.
35. Rosenzweig, *Star*, p. 11.
36. Rosenzweig, *Star*, p. 64; *Stern*, p. 69.
37. Rosenzweig, "Das Neue Denken," p. 386. A discussion of Rosenzweig's critique of philosophy's treatment of time is in Michael D. Oppenheim, "Taking time seriously: An inquiry

into the methods of communication of Soren Kierkegaard and Franz Rosenzweig," *Studies in Religion/Sciences Religieuses* Vol. 7. No. 1 (1978): 53-60.
38. Rosenzweig, *Understanding the Sick and the Healthy,* p. 30.
39. Rosenzweig, *Star,* p. 337.
40. *Ibid.,* p. 47.
41. *Ibid.,* p. 10.
42. Rosenzweig refers to the *Star* as "ein System der Philosophie," in "Das Neue Denken," p. 374.
43. Rosenzweig, *Stern,* p. 3. For an analysis of Rosenzweig's treatment of death see Michael D. Oppenheim, "Death and Man's Fear of Death in Franz Rosenzweig's *The Star of Redemption,*" *Judaism* 108 (Fall 1978): 458-467.
44. Rosenzweig held that the "reductive method" was a primary ingredient of philosophy, because the philosophical mind is not happy until a single principle or element is found that constitutes the whole of reality. God, the world, and man are never allowed to exist as discrete entities. Rosenzweig was able to classify the history of philosophy in terms of the particular reductive principle that was proposed at various times. The three periods of this history are the "cosmological Antiquity," the "theological Middle Ages," and the "anthropological modern era." At first all had been reduced to the world, and then to God, and now philosophy finds its culmination in positing the Self as the primary element. This discussion is found in "Das Neue Denken," p. 378.
45. Rosenzweig, "The New Thinking," *Franz Rosenzweig,* p. 198; "Das Neue Denken," pp. 385-386.
46. Rosenzweig, *Stern,* p. 116.
47. Rosenzweig, *Star,* p. 106.
48. *Ibid.,* pp. 76-77.
49. A comparison of Rosenzweig's treatment of death and that of Martin Heidegger is the focus of the article by Karl Löwith, "M. Heidegger and F. Rosenzweig On Temporality and Eternity," *Philosophy and Phenomenological Research* 3 (1942): 53-77.
50. Rosenzweig, "Das Neue Denken," p. 357.
51. Rosenstock's letter is in Rosenzweig, *Briefe,* quoted in *Judaism Despite Christianity,* pp. 119-120.
52. Rosenzweig, "Das Neue Denken," p. 358.
53. What will be designated at the conclusion of this chapter as the third dimension of revelation, that is, the liturgical dimension,

was treated by Rosenzweig in the *Star* in terms of the category of redemption.
54. Rosenzweig, *Star,* p. 188; *Stern,* p. 209.
55. Rosenzweig, *Star,* p. 390-392; *Stern,* p. 434-436.
56. Rosenzweig, "The New Thinking," p. 207; "Das Neue Denken," p. 398. The term or slogan that Rosenzweig gives to the "New Thinking" is absolute empiricism (*absoluter Empirismus*).
57. Rosenzweig, *Understanding the Sick and the Healthy,* p. 89.
58. Rosenzweig, *Star,* p. 151.
59. *Ibid.,* p. 111.
60. *Ibid.,* p. 147.
61. *Ibid.,* p. 150.
62. *Ibid.*
63. A good analysis of Rosenzweig's philosophy of language is presented by Rivka Horwitz, "Franz Rosenzweig on Language," *Judaism* 13 (1964): 393-406.
64. Rosenzweig, *Star,* p. 178.
65. *Ibid.,* pp. 107-108.
66. *Ibid.,* p. 214.
67. Rosenzweig's idea of human love ensouling the world corresponds to the conception of *"beseelung,"* of Romantic Philosophy. For a discussion of Rosenzweig's debt to Romantic Philosophy see Alexander Altmann, *Studies in Religious Philosophy and Mysticism* (Ithaca: Cornell University Press, 1969), pp. 275 ff.
68. Rosenzweig, *Star,* p. 240.
69. *Ibid.*
70. *Ibid.,* pp. 3-5.
71. Rosenzweig, *Understanding the Sick and the Healthy,* pp. 89-91.
72. Rosenzweig, *Star,* p. 395 and "Urzelle," pp. 366-368.
73. Rosenzweig, *Star,* p. 258.
74. Rosenzweig, *Star,* pp. 296-297; *Stern,* pp. 329-330.

## Chapter 3: Martin Buber

1. Buber refers to the first two stages in the development of his thought in Martin Buber, *Between Man and Man,* Introduction by Maurice Friedman and trans. Ronald Gregor Smith (U.S.: The Macmillan Company, Macmillan Paperbacks Edition, 1965), pp. 184-185. He writes that he was at first under the influence of "German Mysticism," and that later he wrote of a "realization of God through man." Maurice Friedman describes three stages in Buber's thought in Maurice S. Friedman, *Martin Buber: The Life of Dialogue* (Chicago: The University of Chicago Press, 1955), p. 27. Hereafter cited as *Dialogue.* Friedman's more detailed treatment of these stages is in his *Martin Buber's Life and Work: The Early Years 1878-1923* (New York: E.P. Dutton, 1981), hereafter cited as *Life and Work.* Finally, this three-stage characterization is indicated through the chapter headings in Grete Schaeder, *The Hebrew Humanism of Martin Buber,* trans. Noah J. Jacobs (Detroit: Wayne State University Press, 1973). Hereafter cited as *Hebrew Humanism.*
2. Martin Buber, *Pointing the Way: Collected Essays by Martin Buber,* ed. and trans. Maurice S. Friedman (New York: Schocken Books, Schocken Paperback, 1974), ix.
3. Martin Buber, *Daniel: Dialogues on Realization,* trans. with Introduction by Maurice Friedman (New York: McGraw-Hill Book Company, McGraw-Hill Paperback Edition, 1965), p. 95.
4. Martin Buber, *I and Thou,* trans. with Introduction by Walter Kaufmann (New York: Charles Scribner's Sons, 1970), p. 151.
5. Paul Arthur Schilpp and Maurice Friedman, eds., *The Philosophy of Martin Buber,* The Library of Living Philosophers, vol. 12 (La Salle, Illinois: Open Court, 1967), p. 689. Hereafter cited as *Martin Buber.*
6. Martin Buber, *On Judaism,* ed. Nahum N. Glatzer (New York: Schocken Books, Schocken Paperback, 1972), p. 3.
7. Schilpp and Friedman, eds., *Martin Buber,* pp. 4-5.
8. *Ibid.,* p. 4. Also see Schaeder, *Hebrew Humanism,* p. 27.
9. Friedman suggests this in his unpublished dissertation, Maurice S. Friedman, "Martin Buber: Mystic, Existentialist, Social Prophet—A Study in the Redemption of Evil," (Ph.D. dissertation, University of Chicago, 1950), p. 125. Hereafter cited as "Martin Buber." Also see Schaeder, *Hebrew Humanism,* p. 27.

10. For a discussion of the intellectual environment during Buber's early years see Hans Kohn, *Martin Buber, sein Werk und seine Zeit: Ein Versuch über Religion und Politik* (Hellerau: Jakob Hegner Verlag, 1930), pp. 13-55. The youth revolt is discussed in George L. Mosse, *Germans and Jews: The Right, the Left, and the Search for a "Third Force" in Pre-Nazi Germany* (New York: Grosset and Dunlap, The Universal Library, 1970), pp. 77-81. Also see Michael Oppenheim, "Fathers and Sons," *Judaism* 114 (Spring 1980).
11. Oppenheim, "Fathers and Sons."
12. Buber, *Pointing the Way,* ix.
13. Schilpp and Friedman, eds., *Martin Buber,* p. 25.
14. This point is discussed in Friedman, "Martin Buber," p. 82.
15. Martin Buber, *The Legend of the Baal-Shem,* trans. Maurice Friedman (New York: Harper and Brothers, 1955), x. This point is discussed in Friedman, "Martin Buber," p. 40. Buber's own later critical views about his early efforts of creative translation are contained in Friedman, *Life and Work,* pp. 101-5.
16. See Schaeder, *Hebrew Humanism,* pp. 54-60.
17. Martin Buber, "Ueber Jakob Bohme," quoted and translated in Schaeder, *Hebrew Humanism,* p. 61.
18. See discussion in Kohn, *Martin Buber,* pp. 113-116.
19. Martin Buber, *Between Man and Man,* pp. 184-5; Martin Buber, *Werke: Erster Band—Schriften zur Philosophie* (Munich und Heidelberg: Kösel Verlag und Verlag Lambert Schneider, 1962), p. 384. Hereafter cited as *Werke,* Vol. 1.
20. Martin Buber, *Hasidism and Modern Man,* ed. and trans. Maurice Friedman (New York: Harper and Row, Harper Torchbooks, 1966), p. 57.
21. Buber, *Hasidism and Modern Man,* p. 59; Martin Buber, *Werke: Dritter Band—Schriften zum Chassidismus* (Munich und Heidelberg: Kösel Verlag und Verlag Lambert Schneider, 1963), p. 976. Hereafter cited as *Werke,* Vol. 111.
22. Buber, *Hasidism and Modern Man,* p. 77.
23. *Ibid.,* p. 84.
24. *Ibid.,* p. 107.
25. Buber, *Between Man and Man,* p. 184; *Werke,* Vol. 1, p. 384.
26. The first three speeches are contained in Buber, *On Judaism.* These speeches had a strong impact on Zionist circles in Western and Central Europe.
27. Buber, *On Judaism,* p. 27; Martin Buber, *Drei Reden Über Das*

*Judentum* (Frankfurt A/M: Rütten & Loening, 1911), p. 45. Hereafter cited as *Drei Reden*.
28. Buber, *On Judaism*, p. 28; *Drei Reden*, p. 47.
29. The Introduction, "The Teaching of Tao," of Buber's book on Taoism is in Buber, *Pointing the Way*, pp. 31-60; *Werke*, Vol. 1., pp. 1023-1051.
30. See discussion in Kohn, *Martin Buber*, pp. 118-122.
31. Buber, *Pointing the Way*, p. 48.
32. *Ibid.*, p. 45.
33. *Ibid.*, p. 40.
34. Buber, *Daniel;* also see *Werke*, Vol. 1, pp. 7-76.
35. Buber, *Daniel*, p. 136.
36. *Ibid.*
37. *Ibid.*, p. 137.
38. The identification of these three stages follows Erich Przywara, "Judentum und Christentum," *Stimme der Zeit CX* (1925-26), p. 87. The reference to Przywara's article is in Friedman, *Dialogue*, p. 39.
39. Buber, *Daniel*, p. 138.
40. *Ibid.*
41. *Ibid.*, p. 141.
42. *Ibid.*, p. 72.
43. *Ibid.*, 141; *Werke*, Vol. 1, p. 74.
44. Buber, *Daniel*, p. 95.
45. This address is in Buber, *On Judaism*.
46. Buber, *On Judaism*, p. 83.
47. *Ibid.*, p. 81.
48. *Ibid.*, p. 84.
49. *Ibid.*
50. *Ibid.*, p. 87.
51. *Ibid.*, p. 86.
52. *Ibid.*, p. 106.
53. *Ibid.*
54. Buber, *Pointing the Way*, x.
55. The short piece, "With a Monist," is in Buber, *Pointing the Way*. Also see Martin Buber, *Ereignisse und Begegnungen* (Leipzig: Insel Verlag, 1917), pp. 22-36.
56. Buber, *Pointing the Way*, p. 28; *Ereignisse und Begegnungen*, p. 31.
57. Buber, *Pointing the Way*, p. 30.
58. *Ibid.*, p. 29.

59. *Ibid.*
60. Buber, *Daniel,* p. 72.
61. Buber, *Pointing the Way,* p. 27; *Ereignisse und Begegnungen,* p. 29.
62. Buber, *Pointing the Way,* p. 29; *Ereignisse und Begegnungen,* p. 33.
63. "A Conversion" is in Buber, *Between Man and Man,* pp. 13-14.
64. Paul R. Flohr, "The Road to *I and Thou:* An Inquiry into Buber's Transition from Mysticism to Dialogue" in Michael A. Fishbane and Paul R. Flohr, eds., *Texts and Responses: Studies Presented to Nahum N. Glatzer on the Occasion of His Seventieth Birthday by His Students* (Leiden: E.J. Brill, 1975), pp. 201-25.
65. *Ibid.,* p. 218. While Flohr's conclusions about the impact of these letters and conversations are helpful, it is also clear that Buber's thought was in the process of changing independently of the influence of Landauer.
66. Buber, *Between Man and Man,* p. 215.
67. *Ibid.,* pp. 213-5.
68. Buber, *Hasidism and Modern Man,* p. 49. The essay, "My Way to Hasidism," is included in Buber, *Hasidism and Modern Man,* and in *Werke,* Vol. III, pp. 959-73.
69. *Ibid.*
70. *Ibid.*
71. The address, "The Holy Way: A Word to the Jews and to all Nations," is in Buber, *On Judaism.* Hugo Bergman in his essay, "Martin Buber and Mysticism," in Schilpp and Friedman, eds., *Martin Buber,* pp. 302-303, sees this address as a major turning point in Buber's development.
72. Buber, *On Judaism,* p. 109.
73. *Ibid.,* p. 137.
74. *Ibid.,* p. 109.
75. *Ibid.*
76. *Ibid.* p. 110; Martin Buber, *Reden Über Das Judentum* (Berlin: Schocken Verlag, 1932), p. 147. Buber sees true community (*wahre Gemeinschaft*) as the place where God is realized. Hereafter cited as *Reden.*
77. Buber, *On Judaism,* p. 111.
78. *Ibid.,* p. 126.
79. Buber's "Preface" to his addresses, in Buber, *On Judaism,* p. 3.
80. Buber, *On Judaism,* p. 174; *Reden,* p. 235.

81. Buber, *On Judaism*, p. 150.
82. *Ibid.*, p. 156.
83. *Ibid.*, p. 155.
84. *Ibid.*, p. 150.
85. *Ibid.*, p. 155.
86. *Ibid.*, p. 158; *Reden*, p. 213.
87. The first two parts of the three part "Introduction" to *The Great Maggid and His Followers* is in Martin Buber, *The Origin and Meaning of Hasidism*, ed. and trans. Maurice Friedman (New York: Harper & Row, Harper Torchbooks, 1966), pp. 114-149. Hereafter cited as *Origin and Meaning*. Also see Martin Buber, *Der grosse Maggid und seine Nachfolge* (Frankfurt am Main: Rütten und Loening, 1922). Hereafter cited as *Der grosse Maggid*.
88. Buber, *Origin and Meaning*, p. 138.
89. *Ibid.*, p. 126.
90. Buber, *On Judaism*, p. 106.
91. Buber, *Origin and Meaning*, pp. 130-131.
92. *Ibid.*, p. 124.
93. See, for example, Buber, *On Judaism*, pp. 100, 106. Also see Gershom Scholem, *On Jews and Judaism in Crisis: Selected Essays*, ed. Werner J. Dannhauser (New York: Schocken Books, 1976) p. 169. Hereafter cited as *On Jews*. There is a discussion of some of the reasons behind the disagreement between Buber and Scholem concerning Kabbalah and Hasidism in Michael Oppenheim, "The Meaning of Hasidut: Martin Buber and Gershom Scholem" *The Journal of the American Academy of Religion*, No. 3 (September 1981): 410-423.
94. Buber, *Origin and Meaning*, p. 124.
95. *Ibid.*, p. 122.
96. *Ibid.*, p. 116.
97. *Ibid.*, p. 127.
98. *Ibid.*, p. 132.
99. *Ibid.*, p. 134; "Gelectword" to *Der grosse Maggid*, xxxvi-xxxvii.
100. Buber, *Origin and Meaning*, p. 139; *Der grosse Maggid*, xlii.
101. See Rivka Horwitz, *Buber's Way to "I" and "Thou": An Historical Analysis and the First Publication of Martin Buber's Lectures "Religion als Gegenwart"* (Heidelberg: Verlag Lambert Schneider, 1978). Hereafter cited as *Buber's Way*. Friedman's criticisms of Horwitz's views about the nature of Buber's early development and Buber's general philosophy of

dialogue are in his *Life and Work*, pp. 418-20.
102. Horwitz, *Buber's Way,* pp. 92, 103.
203. *Ibid.*, p. 60.
104. Horwitz also speaks of the influence of Ferdinand Ebner on Buber's writing of *I and Thou,* in *Buber's Way,* pp. 170-174.
105. Horwitz, *Buber's Way*, p. 25.
106. "Preface" in Buber, *On Judaism,* pp. 3-10; "Vorrede" to Buber, *Reden*, ix-xix.
107. Buber, *On Judaism*, p. 3.
108. *Ibid.*
109. *Ibid.*, p. 6.
110. *Ibid.*, p. 7.
111. *Ibid.*, p. 5.
112. *Ibid.*, p. 4.
113. *Ibid.*, p. 8.
114. *Ibid.*
115. *Ibid.*
116. *Ibid.*, p. 4.
117. *Ibid.*
118. *Ibid.*
119. *Ibid.*, p. 5.
120. Walter Kaufmann's English translation of *I and Thou* is being used, because it indicates the changes that Buber made to his first edition of *I and Thou*.
121. "Afterword" in Buber, *I and Thou,* p. 171. The "Afterword" was written in 1957, as part of the second German edition of the book. See "Nachwort" in Buber, *Werke,* Vol. I, pp. 161-170.
122. Buber, *I and Thou,* p. 171.
123. *Ibid.*, p. 54.
124. Ludwig Feuerbach, *The Fiery Brook: Selected Writings of Ludwig Feuerbach,* trans. with Introduction by Zawar Hanfi (Garden City, New York: Doubleday & Company, Anchor Books, 1972), p. 244. Buber speaks of Feuerbach's importance in the development of the philosophy of dialogue in *Between Man and Man*, p. 210.
125. Buber, *I and Thou,* p. 62.
126. *Ibid.*, p. 80.
127. *Ibid.*, p. 67.
128. *Ibid.*, p. 81.
129. *Ibid.*, p. 151.
130. The section on revelation is in Buber, *I and Thou,* pp. 157-160;

*Werke,* Vol. I, pp. 152-154.
131. Buber, *I and Thou,* p. 164.
132. *Ibid.,* p. 130.
133. *Ibid.,* p. 134.
134. The "waking dream" is in Buber, *I and Thou,* pp. 120-122: *Werke,* Vol. I, pp. 126-127.
135. Buber, *I and Thou,* pp. 131-143; *Werke,* Vol. I, pp. 134-142.
136. Buber, *I and Thou,* p. 133.
137. *Ibid.*
138. The use of such questions, posed by the reader or some other interlocutor, gives a dynamic dialogical character to the whole work. Although there are no "persons" who are identified by name, the quality of dialogue here is much greater than, for example, in *Daniel.* The sense of timing, of anticipation, and of fairness that motivates these questions in *I and Thou* provides this work with a true sense of dialogue.
139. Buber, *I and Thou,* p. 134.
140. Buber, *I and Thou,* p. 135; *Werke,* Vol. I, pp. 136-137.
141. Buber, *I and Thou,* p. 143.
142. Friedman, *Dialogue,* p. 27.
143. Some of these changes are noted by Scholem in *On Jews,* pp. 145, 151.
144. Buber, *Werke,* Vols. I, II, and III.
145. Buber, *I and Thou,* p. 134.
146. Emil L. Fackenheim, "Martin Buber's Concept of Revelation," in Schilpp and Friedman, eds., *Martin Buber,* p. 284.
147. The section in the first part of *I and Thou,* pp. 60-61, that corresponds to his reference about "spiritual beings" on page 57, discusses art.
148. Buber, *I and Thou,* pp. 60-61. Buber's views about the relationship between his philosophy of dialogue and the realm of art are analyzed in Friedman, *Life and Work,* pp. 328-35. Also see Robert E. Wood, *Martin Buber's Ontology* (Evanston: Northwestern University Press, 1969), pp. 50-1.
149. Buber, *I and Thou,* p. 173.
150. Fackenheim does not note the problem of reciprocity in his defense of the possibility of addressing a tree as "Thou," in "Martin Buber's Concept of Revelation," Schilpp and Friedman, eds., *Martin Buber,* p. 270.
151. Many of Buber's critics have noted the presence of these examples in works that represent various stages in Buber's

development. See, for example: Friedman, *Dialogue*, p. 49; Wood, *Martin Buber's Ontology*, p. 46. Horwitz in *Buber's Way*, pp. 215-216, cites Buber's use of examples from the realms of art and nature in his lectures, "Religion als Gegenwart." Horwitz adds that Buber tried to adapt these examples to the philosophy of dialogue in *I and Thou*.
152. Schaeder, *Hebrew Humanism*, p. 61.
153. *Ibid.*
154. Buber, *Daniel*, p. 54; *Werke*, Vol. I, p. 15.
155. Buber, *I and Thou*, pp. 57-58; *Werke*, Vol. I, 81-82.
156. Friedman's "Introduction" to Buber, *Daniel*, p. 38.
157. Buber, *Daniel*, p. 140; *Werke*, Vol. I, pp. 73-74.
158. Buber, *I and Thou*, pp. 146-147; *Werke*, Vol. I, pp. 144-145.
159. Schaeder, *Hebrew Humanism*, p. 61.
160. Buber, *I and Thou*, pp. 144-145; *Werke*, Vol. I, pp. 143-144.
161. Friedman in *Dialogue*, p. 49, notes that in one case "the emotional content of the experiences as described" in the two works is "almost identical," but he does not draw any conclusions about this.
162. Buber, *I and Thou*, pp. 171-182; *Werke*, Vol. I, pp. 161-170.
163. Buber, *I and Thou*, p. 177.
164. *Ibid.*, p. 173.
165. Scholem, *On Jews*, pp. 126-171, especially see pp. 148-149.
166. The different definitions of mysticism used by Buber and a number of his critics are explored in an article, William E. Kaufman, "The Mysticism of Martin Buber: An Essay on Methodology," *Judaism* 106 (Spring 1978), pp. 175-183. Kaufman holds that Scholem defines mysticism as "an immediate or direct experience of God," p. 177. Throughout the present chapter, Buber's own definition of mysticism has been used.
167. Scholem, *On Jews*, p. 151.
168. *Ibid.*, p. 164.
169. Examples of critics who speak of Buber's pantheism are given in Wood, *Martin Buber's Ontology*, pp. 91, 97. Also see, Charles Hartshorne, "Martin Buber's Metaphysics," Schilpp and Friedman, eds., *Martin Buber*, pp. 49-68.
170. Buber, *I and Thou*, pp. 166-167; *Werke*, Vol. I, p. 158. The German is: "Ob wir Irdischen auch nie Gott ohne Welt, nur die Welt in Gott schauen, schauend bilden wir ewig Gottes Gestalt."
171. Buber, *I and Thou*, p. 127; *Werke*, Vol. I, pp. 130-131. The

German is: "Von der Welt wegblicken, das hilft nicht zu Gott; auf die Welt hinstarren, das hilft auch nicht zu ihm; aber wer die Welt in ihm schaut, steht in seiner Gegenwart."

172. This point is briefly made in a number of places in the text. See, for example, Buber, *I and Thou*, pp. 123, 129. However, there is never an extended discussion. In the "Afterword" to *I and Thou*, p. 181, *Werke*, Vol. I, p. 169, there is an important statement about God's "personhood." Buber writes that the "concept of personhood is, of course, utterly incapable of describing the nature of God; but it is permitted and necessary to say that God is *also* a person." Yet, this addition is made in 1957, and there is no statement about God's personhood in the text itself, not even in the second edition.
173. Buber, *I and Thou*, pp. 157-160; *Werke*, Vol. I, pp. 152-154.
174. *Ibid.*, p. 160; also see p. 157.
175. *Ibid.*, pp. 159-160; *Werke*, Vol. I, pp. 153-154.
176. Schilpp and Friedman, eds., *Martin Buber*, p. 689.

## Chapter 4: Emil Fackenheim

1. Emil L. Fackenheim, *The Jewish Return Into History: Reflections in the Age of Auschwitz and a New Jerusalem* (New York: Schocken Books, 1978), xi-xii. Hereafter cited as *Return*. This statement is reiterated in his later book, *To Mend the World: Foundations of Future Jewish Thought* (New York: Schocken Books, 1982), p. 13. Hereafter cited as *Mend*.
2. Fackenheim's public confrontation with his own experiences in the Nazi camp, Sachenhausen, came in 1975 in an article in the journal *Midstream*. The article is reprinted in *Return*, "Sachenhausen 1938: Groundwork for Auschwitz," pp. 58-67.
3. Fackenheim's article, "An Outline of a Modern Jewish Theology," is in his *Quest for Past and Future: Essays in Jewish Theology* (Boston: Beacon Press, 1970), pp. 96-111. Hereafter cited as *Quest*.
4. *Ibid.*, p. 101.
5. *Ibid*.
6. *Ibid.*, pp. 102-103.
7. *Ibid.*, p. 44.
8. *Ibid.*, p. 105.
9. *Ibid.*, p. 104.
10. *Ibid.*, p. 110.
11. *Ibid.*, p. 101.
12. Soren Kierkegaard (Johannes De Silentio and Anti-Climacus), *Fear and Trembling and The Sickness Unto Death,* trans. with Introductions and Notes by Walter Lowrie (Princeton, New Jersey: Princeton University Press, Princeton Paperback Edition, 1968). If one looks into the dazzling parade of pseudonyms that Kierkegaard employs, it will be seen that Anti-Climacus represents the Christian standpoint in the strongest sense. By using Anti-Climacus to present a powerful portrayal of the limitations of all human endeavors, Kierkegaard can be seen to anticipate one of Fackenheim's later considerations. Both hold that it is only from *within* the standpoint of faith that the despair and tragedy of man's life as lived away from God can be understood.
13. See Oppenheim, "Death and Man's Fear of Death in F. Rosenzweig's *The Star of Redemption.*"
14. Fackenheim, *Quest*, p. 3-26.
15. Dietrich Bonhoeffer, the modern Christian theologian, an-

ticipated Fackenheim's eventual dissatisfaction with theology's effort to prove man's existential sickness in order to bring forth the saving remedy. In a number of his letters from prison he attacked those theologians who used God as a *"Deus ex machina . . . the answer to life's problems, the solution of its distresses and conflicts."* See Dietrich Bonhoeffer, *Letters and Papers from Prison,* ed. Eberhard Bethge and trans. Reginald H. Fuller (New York: The Macmillan Company, Macmillan Paperbacks Edition, 1962), pp. 208-209.
16. Fackenheim, *Quest,* p. 9.
17. It is important to recognize that there is a strong tendency within the Rabbinic tradition to protect the community from the "radical surprise" of encountering God's revelation in the present. The Talmudic story of the oven of Akhnai is a good example of this. This story vividly accentuates the activity of man applying God's word to the world, but the cost of such activism is that the word becomes frozen and a new Voice into the present seems to be foreclosed. The story is from *Bava Metzia* 59b, and is cited in Gershom Scholem, *The Messianic Idea in Judaism: And Other Essays on Jewish Spirituality* (New York: Schocken Books, 1971), pp. 291-2.
18. Fackenheim, *Quest,* p. 10.
19. *Ibid.,* p. 204.
20. *Ibid.,* p. 79.
21. *Ibid.,* pp. 112-3.
22. *Ibid.,* p. 177.
23. *Ibid.,* pp. 250-1.
24. *Ibid.,* p. 281.
25. *Ibid.,* p. 231.
26. *Ibid.,* pp. 229-30.
27. *Ibid.,* p. 243.
28. *Ibid.,* pp. 256, 273, 303. See, also, Fackenheim, "Man and His World in the Perspective of Judaism," *Judaism* (Spring 1967): 174.
29. Fackenheim, *Quest,* p. 273.
30. *Ibid.,* p. 303.
31. *Ibid.,* p. 315.
32. *Ibid.,* p. 19.
33. In Fackenheim, *Mend,* p. 10, Fackenheim writes that he first understood the uniqueness of the threat of the Holocaust to Jewish belief during a symposium in the Spring of 1967.

34. Fackenheim, "Hope," pp. 100-101. Fackenheim often abandons philosophical discourse in order to draw upon *midrashim,* Jewish stories and interpretations. He believes that stories are able to bring to the surface things that he and other theologians can only inadequately struggle with. He is especially fond of quoting from the novels of Elie Wiesel, who himself acknowledges his own impotence in the face of what should be said about the Holocaust and its place in Jewish self-understanding.
35. Fackenheim, *God's Presence,* p. 72.
36. *Ibid.*
37. Fackenheim, "Hope," p. 87.
38. Fackenheim, *God's Presence,* p. 76.
39. *Ibid.,* p. 70.
40. *Ibid.* There is a more detailed treatment of this issue of uniqueness in *Mend,* pp. 12-13.
41. Fackenheim's emphasis on the *uniqueness* of the Holocaust is an extremely important element in his attempt to uncover the *theological* meaning of this event. In speaking of the Holocaust's uniqueness, he is undermining any attempts to explain the event in terms of the categories of sociology, political science, or history. Fackenheim holds that as a unique event it can only be seen within one context: the singled-out Jewish condition. On the other hand, Richard Rubenstein, who rejects the idea of a personal God who directs history, insists on looking at the Holocaust in terms of the politics of power. This position is forcefully presented in Richard L. Rubenstein, *The Cunning of History: The Holocaust and the American Future* (New York: Harper & Row, Harper Colophon Books, 1978).
42. In Fackenheim, *Mend,* p. 234, Fackenheim expresses reservations about the usefulness of the category of radical evil.
43. Fackenheim, *God's Presence,* pp. 8-14.
44. *Ibid.* p. 6.
45. *Ibid.,* p. 16.
46. Emil L. Fackenheim, "Jewish Values in the Post-Holocuast Future: A Symposium," *Judaism* 16 (1967): 269-273, additional comments are made by Fackenheim, 284-295. Hereafter cited as "Symposium."
47. *Ibid.* In response to a statement by Elie Wiesel, who also participated in this symposium, Fackenheim retracted his earlier statement that brought out the parallels between the destruction

of the two temples and the Holocaust.
48. See, for example: Seymour Cain, "The Questions and the Answers After Auschwitz," *Judaism* 20 (1971): 263-278; Michael Wyschogrod, "Faith and the Holocaust," *Judaism* 20 (1971): 286-294; and, more recently, Arthur A. Cohen, "On Emil Fackenheim's *To Mend the World:* A Review Essay," *Modern Judaism* (May 1983): 225-236.
49. Fackenheim, *God's Presence,* pp. 8-14.
50. *Ibid.,* p. 13.
51. *Ibid.,* p. 88.
52. Fackenheim, "Symposium," p. 284.
53. Fackenheim, *God's Presence,* p. 88.
54. *Ibid.,* p. 95.
55. *Ibid.,* p. 84.
56. *Ibid.,* p. 15.
57. Fackenheim, "Hope," p. 101.
58. Fackenheim, *God's Presence,* p. 88.
59. *Ibid.,* p. 83.
60. Fackenheim, "Symposium," p. 272. He discusses and provides a revised view of this Voice and commandment in *Mend,* pp. 24, 26, 300.
61. Fackenheim, "Symposium," p. 295.
62. *Ibid.,* p. 272.
63. Fackenheim, *God's Presence,* p. 84. He had written about the Jewish duty to survive as early as 1959. See *Quest,* p. 125.
64. Fackenheim, *God's Presence,* pp. 85-86.
65. *Ibid.,* p. 86.
66. Fackenheim, *Quest,* p. 19.
67. *Ibid.*
68. Fackenheim, "Symposium," p. 273.
69. Fackenheim, *God's Presence,* pp. 95-96.
70. *Ibid.,* p. 76.
71. *Ibid.,* p. 78.
72. *Ibid.,* p. 79.
73. *Ibid.,* p. 31.
74. Fackenheim, *Return,* p. 279.
75. *Ibid.,* p. 26.
76. *Ibid.,* p. 286.
77. He holds in *Mend,* pp. 24-25, that Jews can obey the commanding Voice in our time only because Jews resisted the Nazis during the Holocaust.

78. Fackenheim, *Mend,* p. 262.
79. *Ibid.,* p. 23. Fackenheim has moved farther and farther away from a style of neutrality since he has seriously examined the Holocaust.
80. *Ibid.,* p. 20. Previous to this he only believed that Jewish thought had to be self-exposed to history.
81. Fackenheim, *Quest,* p. 63.
82. Emil L. Fackenheim, *Encounters Between Judaism and Modern Philosophy: A Preface to Future Jewish Thought* (New York: Basic Books, 1973), p. 213.
83. *Ibid.,* p. 228.
84. Fackenheim, *Mend,* pp. 166-167.
85. *Ibid.,* p. 253. The encounter with the Holocaust has brought two other important contemporary Jewish thinkers to utilize the concepts of Jewish mysticism. See Richard L. Rubenstein, *After Auschwitz: Radical Theology and Contemporary Judaism* (Indianapolis: Bobbs-Merrill Company, 1966), pp. 217-225, and Arthur A. Cohen, *The Tremendum: A Theological Interpretation of the Holocaust* (New York: Crossroad, 1981).
86. Fackenheim, *Mend,* pp. 250-255.
87. *Ibid.,* p. 276.
88. *Ibid.,* p. 277.
89. *Ibid.,* p. 267.
90. *Ibid.,* pp. 279, 284.
91. *Ibid.,* p. 289.
92. *Ibid.,* pp. 225-230.
93. *Ibid.,* p. 300.
94. *Ibid.,* p. 312.
95. *Ibid.,* pp. 145, 304, 312-313.
96. In his earlier writings Fackenheim had said that no saving or redeeming Voice can be found in connection with the Holocaust. See "Hope," pp. 100-101, and *God's Presence,* p. 88.

# Chapter 5: Conclusion

1. Rosenzweig, *Star,* p. 93.
2. This phrase is the title of the book, James Collins, *The Emergence of Philosophy of Religion* (New Haven: Yale University Press, 1967).
3. Alfred North Whitehead, *Religion In The Making* (Cleveland: The World Publishing Company, Meridian Books, 1960), p. 16.
4. Rosenzweig, "The New Thinking," p. 198.
5. Rosenzweig, *Star,* pp. 296-297; *Stern,* pp. 329-330.
6. Fackenheim, *Quest,* p. 5.
7. As we saw in Chapter Two, Rosenzweig describes this contact between God and man under the category of redemption.
8. Fackenheim, *Return,* p. 189. Rosenzweig's view of Judaism that takes it out of human history is the most alienating feature of his thought for contemporary Jews and Jewish thinkers.
9. Franz Rosenzweig, *On Jewish Learning* (New York: Schocken Books, 1965), p. 118. This quotation is from a letter of Rosenzweig of 1924, which is contained in *Briefe,* pp. 518-521.
10. *Ibid.,* pp. 120-124.
11. *Ibid.,* p. 85. This quotation is from Rosenzweig's letter to Buber of 1923, which is titled "Die Bauleute" ("The Builders"), and contained in *Kleinere Schriften,* pp. 106-121.
12. *Ibid.,* pp. 85-86.
13. *Ibid.,* p. 83.
14. Buber, *I and Thou,* p. 189.
15. See, for example, Gershom Scholem's "Martin Buber's Conception of Judaism," *On Jews,* pp. 126-171.
16. This is from a letter to Rosenzweig from Buber, which is included in Rosenzweig, *On Jewish Learning,* p. 111.
17. *Ibid.,* p. 115.
18. Fackenheim, *Quest,* p. 110.

# Index

*Addresses on Judaism,* 53-4, 57-8, 61-4, 67-8, 97

Bonhoeffer, Dietrich, 144-5
Buber, Martin, 3-4, 10, 45-85, 91, 94, 106, 117-8, 120, 123, 125-6; dialogue, 10, 69-72, 76-9, 82, 84-5, 141; *Erlebnis* (experience), 60-1, 63, 68, 82; Fackenheim on, 77; Hasidism, 47, 51-3, 57-8, 61, 64-6; Jewish philosophy, 7-11; meeting, 64-5, 77-9; mutuality (see reciprocity); mysticism, 4, 10, 46, 48-53, 62-3, 72-6, 82, 117-8, 120; realization, 46, 52-62, 66, 68, 79; reciprocity, 70-2, 76-8, 82; revelation, 71-2, 83-4, 123, 125-6; romanticism, 4, 48, 56; and Rosenzweig, 67; Zionism, 51
"Builders, The," 124-5

Cohen, Hermann, 20

*Daniel,* 54-7, 79
Descartes, Rene, 90

Fackenheim, Emil, 4-5, 87-114, 118-23, 126-8; Auschwitz and Jerusalem, 105, 107-8, 112; and Buber, 91, 94, 106; Christianity, 111; existentialism, 4, 109-10, 118-21; Holocaust, 4, 10, 88, 93-114; Holocaust and its uniqueness, 98, 145-6; Israel (see Auschwitz and Jerusalem); Jewish philosophy, 7-11; Jewish tradition, 111; Jew's singled-out condition, 92-4; *midrash,* 8, 146; Philosophy, 110-1; revelation, 92, 121-3; on Rosenzweig, 122-3; *Tikkun* (mending), 108-14, 121; voice of God in Auschwitz, 4, 97, 101-8; vulnerability to history, 4, 87-8, 109, 121-3
Feuerbach, Ludwig, 70
Flohr, Paul (Mendes-Flohr), 60-1
*Freies Jüdisches Lehrhaus,* 24-5
Freud, Sigmund, 6
Friedman, Maurice, 76

*God's Presence in History,* 99-103

Halacha (Jewish Law), 90, 123-8
Hegel, G.W.F., 5-6, 9, 15, 27-8, 32
Heidegger, Martin, 109-10
Heschel, Abraham, 1
History, 35, 87-8, 109, 121-3
Horwitz, Rivka, 66-7
Hume, David, 6

*I and Thou,* 66-7, 69-85, 91, 125-6, 141

Modern Jewish philosophy, 7-9

*Jewish Return into History,* 87

Kierkegaard, Soren, 13-4, 90-1, 144

Landauer, Gustav, 60-1
Language, philosophy of, 37-40, 71

"New Thinking, The," 26, 36-7
Nietzsche, Friedrich, 5, 34, 83

*Quest for Past and Future*, 88-95

Rosenstock, Eugen (Rosenstock-Huessy), 15-21, 34
Rosenzweig, Franz, 3, 9-10, 13-44, 116-7, 119-20, 122-5, 128; Christianity, 15-20, 35, 42; death, man's fear of, 31, 34, 41, 133; Jewish community, 25, 42-3; Jewish philosophy, 7-10; language, 37-40; liturgy, 18-20, 42-3; meeting, 18, 30-2; Meinecke, letter to, 22-5; neighbor, 40-2; Philosopher/Theologian, 43-4, 119-20; Philosophy, 3, 25-44, 116-7, 119-20, 133; redemption, 39-41, 43; revelation, 20-1, 27, 32, 34-6, 39-44, 122-3; time, 29-30, 42-3; Yom Kippur experience, 18-20
Rubenstein, Richard, 146

Scholem, Gershom, 82, 139
*Star of Redemption*, 19, 21-2, 26 28-44, 91, 115, 119

Tillich, Paul, 91
*To Mend the World*, 108-112

*Understanding the Sick and the Healthy*, 25-6, 37

Wiesel, Elie, 101, 146

SYMPOSIUM SERIES

1. Jurgen Moltman *et al.*, **Religion and Political Society**
2. James Grace, editor, **God, Sex, and the Social Project: The Glassboro Papers on Religion and Human Sexuality**
3. M. Darrol Bryant and Herbert Richardson, editors, **A Time for Consideration: A Scholarly Appraisal of the Unification Church**
4. Donald G. Jones, editor, **Private and Public Ethics: Tensions Between Conscience and Institutional Responsibility**
5. Herbert Richardson, editor, **New Religions and Mental Health: Understanding the Issues**
6. Sheila Greeve Davaney, editor, **Feminism and Process Thought: The Harvard Divinity School/Claremont Center for Process Studies Symposium Papers**
7. International Movement, A.T.D./Fourth World, **Children of Our Time: The Children of the Fourth World**
8. Jenny Hammett, **Woman's Transformations: A Psychological Theology**
9. S. Daniel Breslauer, **A New Jewish Ethics**
10. Darrell J. Fasching, editor, **The Jewish People in Christian Preaching**
11. Henry Vander Goot, **Interpreting the Bible in Theology and the Church**
12. Everett Ferguson, **Demonology of the Early Christian World**
13. Marcia Sachs Littell, editor, **Holocaust Education: A Resource Book for Teachers and Professional Leaders**
14. Char Miller, editor, **Missions and Missionaries in the Pacific**
15. John S. Peale, **Biblical History as the Quest for Maturity**
16. Joseph A. Buijs, editor, **Christian Marriage Today: Growth or Breakdown?**
17. Michael Oppenheim, **What Does Revelation Mean for the Modern Jew?**